What do you expect?

Ecclesiastes for Today

Melvin Tinker

EP BOOKS
Faverdale North
Darlington
DL3 0PH, England

web: http://www.epbooks.org

e-mail: sales@epbooks.org

EP Books are distributed in the USA by:
JPL Distribution
3741 Linden Avenue Southeast
Grand Rapids, MI 49548
E-mail: orders@jpldistribution.com
Tel: 877.683.6935

British Library Cataloguing in Publication Data available

ISBN 978–1–78397–006–3

Printed in the UK by Bell & Bain Ltd, Glasgow

This book is dedicated to two special and lasting friends
Paul and Louise

Contents

Preface

The Book of Ecclesiastes both fascinates and captivates. Herman Melville in *Moby Dick*, described Ecclesiastes as 'the truest of all books', this 'fine hammered steel of woe.' George Bernard Shaw compared it to Shakespeare. Ernest Hemingway was entranced by the book. His novel *The Sun Also Rises* uses as an epigraph the book's opening poem. A character in John Updike's *Rabbit* trilogy describes Ecclesiastes as 'the Lord's last word.' Even the band, U2 used it as an inspiration for its song *The Wanderer*.

Also contemporary film reflects some of the musings of Ecclesiastes, how at one moment life feels so worthwhile especially in the face of beauty, but within a heartbeat fades into grey and hollow emptiness. 'There is perhaps no better example than the 1999 Academy Award-winning movie American Beauty which calls into question our contemporary obsession with producing "beauty" while simultaneously suggesting that there is another more fragile beauty that is present for those who have eyes to

see it. Lester's voice-over at the movie's beginning and end
serves in a similar way to the opening and closing poems
of Ecclesiastes, bookending what happens in between:
"It's hard to stay mad when there's so much beauty in the
world … I can't feel anything but gratitude for every single
moment of my stupid little life."[1]

Not only is this a fascinating book, which has sense of
timelessness about it, it is also a controversial book. The
controversy lies in how to read it. Is it to be read as a deeply
pessimistic take on life or a more positive affirmation of
life—especially in eating and drinking? Is it a book for the
pessimist or the hedonist?

As we shall see, the writer is far too unique a thinker to be
neatly pigeonholed. While we must be careful not to make
him into a '21st Century man', much of what he says does
seem to be remarkably contemporary—'postmodern' even,
as it wrestles with paradox and contradictions, happily
holding them together without feeling the need to apologise
for the fact. He may make us feel rather disorientated in that
he does not adopt a straight, linear style of argumentation,
but tends to go back and forth—even sideways at times—in
his themes and observations. Ecclesiastes draws us into his
own spiritual journey as he explores the meaning of life, not
by way of abstract philosophy (although there is much here
philosophers would do well to consider), but by personal
observation and experiment. Much of what he says will
resonate with the modern reader, whether Christian or not.
One thing is for sure, a careful reading of this book will
result in us never seeing the world in the same way again.

It would be a mistake, however, to view these writings
as merely the contemplations of an ancient king with time

on his hands and money to spare. For this is a book which is one with 65 other books which make up the Bible. It is therefore part of a bigger story which culminates in the greatest story ever told centring upon a descendent of Ecclesiastes—Jesus Christ. As we shall see, many of the questions the writer wrestles with find their resolution in the man from Nazareth (who is also the God from heaven) and this makes all the difference in the world. Whether a Christian believer or not, if you have a sneaking suspicion that life is meant to be more than what we wear, eat, drink, work and play, and yet no matter what you do you are still left with a sense of incompleteness, then read on, this is the book for you.

I would like to express my deepest gratitude to so many people for making this book possible.

First, a great note of thanks to Mark Lanier for his kind generosity in enabling me to use the excellent facilities of the Lanier Theological Library in Houston, Texas. Mark is one of the most personable, kindest and ablest men I have ever met and his vision in setting up such a wonderful resource is truly inspiring. I would like to thank the library's staff, including Charles Mickey the library's Director, Sharon Cofran, the chief librarian and all the other wonderful ladies of the library, 'Southern belles', every one of them; one could not wish for a more gracious and helpful staff team.

Secondly, I would like to express my gratitude to Shirley Godbold for her labour of love in checking over the manuscript and to my colleague Dr Richard Hawes, for his review of the many references. Appreciation is also expressed to Philip Tinker and the questions he has produced at the end of each chapter for further thought and discussion.

It continues to be a great source of joy to belong to a church, St John, Newland, which loves the teaching of the Bible, and more importantly, the God of the Bible. Thanks also to my ministerial colleagues whose faithful Biblical teaching continues to inspire and challenge me— Lee McMunn, Scott Mckay and Jake Belder.

Finally, as always, my heartfelt thanks goes to my wife Heather who remains my most loyal supporter, critic and friend.

Soli Deo Gloria,

Melvin Tinker
The Lanier Library, Houston, Texas

1

Bubbles and smoke

Ecclesiastes 1:1–11

Here are the anguished words of a fourteen year old schoolgirl:

Why am I here? What have I done? Why was I born? Who cares about me? I am me. I must suffer because I am me. Why do we live? For love, for happiness? Why should I not commit suicide? I hate this world. I hate my parents and my home— though why, I do not know. I searched for truth, but I only found uncertainty. I was thwarted in my search for love. Where can I find happiness? I do not know. Perhaps I shall never know.[2]

You would have to possess a heart of stone not to be moved by those sentiments, but I suspect that such angst-ridden thoughts are only going to become increasingly more common as society continues to fragment with a descent into the superficial and as parents, politicians and teachers fail to face up to the big questions in life. Although touched by this heartfelt cry of a young girl we are probably not all that surprised, after all, letters in the 'Agony Aunt' columns of teenage magazines and TV documentaries express similar cries.

But just in case we might be tempted to dismiss such thoughts as being the misplaced musings of modern youth, here are similar sentiments from someone of quite a different generation belonging to a different age:

> My question, the one that brought me to the point of suicide when I was fifty years old, was a most simple one that lies in the soul of every person, from a silly child to a wise old man. It is the question without which life is impossible, as I had learnt from experience. It is this: what will come of what I do today or tomorrow? What will come of my entire life?
>
> Expressed another way the question can be put like this: why do I live? Why do I wish for anything, or do anything? Or expressed another way: is there any meaning in my life that will not be annihilated by the inevitability of death which awaits me?[3]

Those words were written by the author of *War and Peace*, Leo Tolstoy.

To complete our 'trilogy of desperation', let us hear the words of a modern writer—Tom Wolfe:

> The whole conviction of my life now rests upon the belief that the sense of loneliness, far from being a rare and curious

phenomenon peculiar to myself and to a few solitary people, is the central and inevitable fact of human existence. All this hideous doubt, despair, and dark confusion of the soul a lonely person must know; for he is united to no image save which he creates himself. He is bolstered by no other knowledge save that which he can gather himself with the vision of his own eyes and brain. He is sustained and cheered and aided by no party. He is given comfort by no creed. He has no faith in him except his own and often that faith deserts him leaving him shaken and filled with impotence. Then it seems to him that his life has come to nothing. That he is ruined, lost, and broken past redemption and that morning, that bright and shining morning with its promise of new beginnings, will never come upon the earth again as it once did.[4]

What may come as a surprise is when we read similar words in the Bible. Indeed, the whole of the book of Ecclesiastes appears at first sight to be one long variation on the same despairing theme of the troubled teenager, Tolstoy and Wolfe (although as we shall discover it is so much more). We only have to consider the opening few verses which afford a taste of what is to come: 'Meaningless, meaningless' says the Teacher, 'Utterly meaningless! Everything is meaningless.' It sounds so 'irreligious', so 'un-Christian', so 'heretical' and yet here it is repeated over and over again like a haunting refrain. Little wonder that Medieval Old Testament scholars called Ecclesiastes one of the Bible's 'two dangerous books.'! (The other one being the Song of Solomon with its overt sexuality).[5]

We have to admit that the thoughts and observations of our writer do appear to have a contemporary ring about them, chiming in with the views of many modern writers and thinkers. In fact they resonate with the thoughts and feelings of the ordinary man and woman in the street. In other words, the world our writer inhabits with all its disappointments, frustrations and contradictions—where so much is expected and so little delivered, and yet at the same time with the awareness that there is much in life which makes it worth living, is very much *our* world. However, we would be wrong to draw the conclusion that this book has found its way into the Bible by mistake, that somehow an atheist has managed to slip one by the compilers of Scripture! For what soon becomes apparent is that this man is a firm believer in the one true God.[6]

When reading commentaries on Ecclesiastes we often come across statements like these:

> This book … is one of the most difficult books in the Bible to read and to understand. Its interest is no less significant a subject than the meaning of life.[7]

> Ecclesiastes is perhaps the most enigmatic book in the Old Testament. Like the desert Sphinx, it teases us with questions, yields its secrets only grudgingly, and will not allow us the luxury of easy answers. In other words, it is thoroughly irritating, but at the same time almost mesmeric in its appeal.[8]

> Ecclesiastes poses one of the more interesting hermeneutical [interpretive] challenges in the Old Testament, for two reasons. First, the message of the book seems to be at odds with theological trajectories evident elsewhere in the Hebrew

Scriptures. Second, at least on the surface, Ecclesiastes is dotted with noticeable internal inconsistencies.[9]

Trying to grasp Ecclesiastes feels like trying to pin down a large resistant octopus; just when you think you have the tentacles under control, there is one sticking out again![10]

A daunting book indeed! However, because something is difficult to understand doesn't mean it is impossible. We shall see that once we have grasped a few basic principles we will find this to be a book which is pastorally helpful and apologetically useful (even though answers are not yielded all that easily!). It is a book which helps Christians connect with unbelievers who are living in the same good but broken, messed up world we are all in, struggling for answers. We shall discover that, in the words of G. K. Chesterton, 'Not only are we in the same boat, but we are all seasick.'[11] What is more, it enables people to see the world as *God* sees it and so to do something about it. This idea of seeing things properly, taking the time to look at life squarely in the face, is fundamental to the writer's outlook.[12] It is not a matter of approaching life with all its beauty and ugliness with our own preconceived ideas, airbrushing out what we consider awkward or inconvenient, but engaging in a comprehensive survey of life and following through whatever clues there may be to where they might lead.

The person
Who, then, is the writer of this enigmatic yet enticing book and what can we know about him?

The first thing to say is that the one who has put the book

together is *not* the same person who came up with the
teaching in the first place. The compiler, or 'frame narrator',
has come along later to put the author's words down in
some sort of order, giving shape to his teaching as well as
giving his own assessment of the project. This is indicated
by the use of the third person to describe the author as 'The
Teacher' (Ecclesiastes 1:1; 7:27; 12:8). Furthermore, at the end
of the work the compiler adds his own comments about 'The
Teacher', 'Not only was the Teacher wise, but he imparted
knowledge to the people' (Ecclesiastes 12:9–14). But this still
leaves us with the question: what can we know about the man
who had wrestled with some of life's big questions and who
seemed to live on the edge?

There are a number of things we can deduce about him.

In the first place, as we have seen, he is described as
'The Teacher'. The term is 'Qoheleth' (pronounced ko-he-
leth), which is associated with the word for 'assembly',
'congregation' or even (at the risk of anachronism) 'church'.[13]
Here, then, is someone who is used to gathering people
around him in order to instruct them. It may be that he had
such a reputation for this sort of activity that the term, 'The
Teacher' became a substitute for his own personal name.
This is not all that unusual. For example, one of the most
influential preachers of the 20th century was Dr Martyn
Lloyd-Jones. He was often simply referred to as 'the Doctor.'
It may well be that something like that is happening here.

The term Qoheleth may in fact have a double meaning.
Not only is this a person who 'gathers' people around him in
order to instruct, he 'gathers' teaching material and insights
for instruction. This is a man of many talents.

As a preacher his teaching method is both enticing and

disconcerting. We in the West tend to engage in a linear development of an argument, mainly because we are used to so-called 'scientific reasoning'. We are very much 'left brain' people; anatomical, atomistic, even mechanical in our thinking. But the Teacher is more of a poet who tends to circle around a theme, develop it, toy with it, even appearing contradictory at times; very much a user of the right hemisphere of the brain. This is someone who 'understands subtlety, nuance, ambiguity, irony and metaphor. It lives with the complexities the left brain tries to resolve by breaking them down into their component parts.'[14] Indeed, from a formal philosophical viewpoint, the Teacher saws off the branch upon which he is sitting for if *everything* is 'meaningless', this includes the contents of this book, in which case the writer is 'self-referentially refuting' and we can safely ignore what he says!

Early in the book, we hear the Teacher speaking of wisdom which starts out to be so full of promise:

> I saw that wisdom is better than folly,
> just as light is better than darkness.
> The wise man has eyes in his head,
> while the fool walks in the darkness (Ecclesiastes 2:14a).

So far so good we might think, but then he seems to ditch it all by going on to say,

> but I came to realise
> that the same fate has overtaken them both.
> Then I thought in my heart
> 'The fate of the fool will overtake me also.

What then do I gain from being wise?'
I said in my heart, 'This too is meaningless'
(Ecclesiastes 2:14b–15).

He really does seem to know how to put the mockers on things! However, a moment's thought reveals that he is being cleverly subtle, as his teaching *style* reflects the *content* of his teaching, expressing what life often *feels* like—the feeling that you are making progress, maybe in an experiment or a relationship, and then the rug is pulled right from underneath your feet and you are left high and dry wondering, 'How did that happen? What's the point?'

To put it bluntly, the writer is saying that life is messy. This is what his style of argument demonstrates. There is no straightforwardness or progression in his method of argumentation. Form follows content. We find that the book will often double back on itself, picking up life's contradictory elements. So, wisdom is both useless and better than foolishness. Life is pointless and yet precious. We are to enjoy life's gifts yet recognise that they are vain. What the writer gives us with one hand, he often takes back with the other. After all, he recognises, 'How can anyone straighten out what God has made crooked?' (7:13; cf. 1:14–15).

Reading Ecclesiastes brings to mind a classic cartoon which has an editor looking over a manuscript and saying, 'Mr Dickens, either it was the best of times or it was the worst of times. It can't be both.' Ecclesiastes is saying, life *is* like that, it is both, riddled with paradox and contradiction, it is very messy and I aim to prove it to you.

Accordingly, reading Ecclesiastes may prove a little frustrating, but that may be because we live in an age where we want and expect all the answers to be delivered in an instant. We have immediate access to a world-wide encyclopaedia at the touch of a keypad. Do you have a question? Simple, 'Google' the answer. But then, what we are given is second-hand, pre-digested factual material and often designed to meet our immediate needs ('Which restaurant should I dine out in tonight?' 'Which film is being shown at the cinema?'). But the things which are worthwhile and lasting don't often yield themselves to us without effort on our part. Sometimes a long, steep climb up a mountain might appear unappealing at the outset, but the view from the top proves to be spectacular and confirms that the climb was worthwhile after all. Our writer is a consummate hiker and guide. He is worth following.

This is the way this kind of literature (wisdom) works. It is not the way of following a formal argument; it is an invitation to see through the eyes of another, to adopt a different angle of vision which enables new perspectives to be gained. It is like embarking on a journey as a fellow traveller with someone pointing things out along the way and sharing his insights as well as asking questions in the hope that some of them will be discovered together. This does not mean there is no formal literary structure to the writing, there is, but the way it is followed is not by following the normal 'Western' rules of argumentation.[15]

The teaching can be divided into two categories: observation and instruction, which tend to alternate with each other. For example, chapter 1:3 through to chapter 4:16 forms one long 'observation complex', viewing what happens in a wide variety of situations and then going on to draw conclusions (usually that it is all 'meaningless'!). This is followed by chapter 5 where wise advice is offered such as:

Do not be quick with your mouth,
do not be hasty in your heart
to utter anything before God.
God is in heaven
and you are on earth,
so let your words be few.
As a dream comes when there are many cares,
so the speech of a fool when there are many words.

(Ecclesiastes 5:2–3)

Here is a Teacher *par excellence,* interesting, intriguing and insightful.

In the second place, we are informed that he is a 'son of David, king of Israel'. Not surprisingly some have identified the writer as King Solomon whom we know was called a 'wise man'.[16] This is the Bible's assessment of him:

God gave Solomon wisdom and very great insight, and a breadth of understanding as measureless as the sand on the seashore. Solomon's wisdom was greater than the wisdom of all the men of the East, and greater than all the wisdom of Egypt.

(1 Kings 4:29–30).

Other scholars consider him to be a descendent of Solomon who appears a little later on in Israel's history. This is suggested by the kind of language used, but nonetheless he still appears to be very much a 'chip off the old block', a thinker. The fact that he was King puts him at the centre of the life of Israel. This means he is not some ivory-towered academic out of reach and out of touch, but someone who has to get on with the business of government. What is more, as King he was in part responsible for ensuring that Israel's religious life stayed on track. In other words, this is a believer in Israel's one true God involved in the rough and tumble of everyday life. This is someone we can connect with.[17]

The proposition

'Meaningless! Meaningless!' says the Teacher. 'Utterly meaningless! Everything is meaningless.' What does man gain from all his labour at which he toils under the sun?
(Ecclesiastes 1:2–3).

There are three things regarding this fundamental proposition we need to understand as they provide us with the appropriate keys for unlocking the rest of the book.

First, the term translated 'meaningless', or as the Authorised, King James Version renders it, 'Vanity', appears 38 times in Ecclesiastes. The NIV translation doesn't really do justice to the word because the Teacher goes on to talk about plenty of things which *do* have some measure of meaning such as work, serving God, enjoying God's good gifts like eating and drinking. The Hebrew word is *hebel*, (pronounced 'hevel'). What the line says is, '*Hebel! Hebel!*' says the teacher 'Everything is *hebel*'. It is a word linked to the tragic figure of 'Abel' whose life was cut short by the murderous actions of his brother Cain (Genesis 4). He didn't live long enough to reach his full potential; his life was 'nasty, brutish and short'. It therefore does not quite mean 'meaningless' as we tend to understand the term. Iain Provan puts it this way:

It is certainly true that to translate *hebel* as 'meaningless' as the NIV does, causes serious difficulties for the interpretation of the book as a unified work, for even a cursory reading of Ecclesiastes demonstrates that Qohelet [the teacher] does not consider everything meaningless. On the contrary he is constantly to be found recommending certain ways of being to his listeners precisely because it is possible for human beings to know the goodness and joy of existence (cf. 2:24–26; 3:12–13, 22). 'Everything' is not 'meaningless'.[18]

It is probably easier to *show* what *hebel* means rather than attempting to define it precisely.

If you were to take a pair of spectacles and breathe on them, what happens? A thin film of vapour appears and then just as quickly vanishes. That is *hebel*. It can be rendered 'breath', 'mist' or even 'smoke' (hence, Eugene Petersen's paraphrase of the Bible, *The Message,* 'Smoke, smoke everything is smoke'). It is a word which depicts that 'here today, gone tomorrow' experience of things. This is what so much of life seems like, ephemeral, short lived. You may enter into a relationship which you think is going to last and suddenly it is cut short either by infidelity or death and it is gone like a puff of smoke. Or maybe you embark upon a career in which you think you are going to leave your mark, only to look back as the years have flown by with retirement just around the corner, and you are left feeling that you have achieved so little, wondering, 'Is this it?' That is *hebel*—vapour.[19]

Another illustration which helps to give a feel of *hebel* would be the nature of soap bubbles. This is the trick little children fall for time and time again. You blow some bubbles and say, 'Go ahead and catch them'. In their trusting innocence they try to do just that and the moment they put out their small hand to grasp the bubble—'pop'—it is gone. That is *hebel*. This is linked to another favourite phrase used by the writer to describe our experience, a 'chasing after the wind.' How can you catch the wind? If you caught it, it wouldn't be moving and so it wouldn't be the wind. So much in life *feels* like that, it is elusive. You think that have something in your grasp, that sense of having 'arrived' and then, 'pop' it disappears. What is more, the *whole* of life can appear to be that way.

If this picture holds true, that much in life, or life as a whole, is like a chasing after bubbles, then another dimension is introduced, that of 'absurdity'. It would be a patently absurd situation to have a grown man or woman spending all their waking hours literally chasing after bubbles. But if, at rock bottom, this is what life really amounts to, then absurdity would not be too strong a word to describe humankind's sad enterprise. Hence, Peter Enns' translation of verses 2–4, 'Utterly absurd … utterly absurd, everything is absurd. What profit is there in anyone's labour under the sun? A generation goes [dies] and another one comes; the world remains unchanged.'[20] He summarises the argument of chapter 1 in these terms: 'Everything, and I mean everything, is absurd. No matter what you do, you have ultimately nothing to show for it. You live and then you die.'[21]

In summary, *hebel* means that life is *ephemeral,* here today gone tomorrow and *elusive,* impossible to pin down.

The second phrase we need to understand is 'gain' (*yitron*) which could equally be rendered 'profit' or 'surplus'—a return for your investment, together with the associated term 'toil' (*hamal*). For example, 1:3, 'What does man *gain* from all his labour at which he *toils*?' The Teacher is asking: 'Is there a bottom line to life?' It is a word normally associated with the financial world, here the question is being asked: can we really be sure of success in life? Furthermore, we are not to fool ourselves into thinking that any of this will come to us handed on a plate; it will more often than not involve plenty of 'blood, sweat and tears'—toil. The big question however, is: will it all be worth it? For many the answer will be 'no'. 'The mass of men', said Henry Thoreau, 'lead lives of quiet desperation.'[22]

Of course, for many their lives are far from being *quietly* desperate. A large proportion of the human race barely reaches adulthood, with most living from day to day trying to eke out a meagre existence. We in the West are often cushioned from such things as famine, war and disease, but not many people in the world experience this. We may think of the plight of the Sudanese; their lot is that of Ecclesiastes with a vengeance. But in so many different ways even we in the West can hit a brick wall when it comes to the 'bottom line' of life, as Thoreau's observation notes. Here is an extract from an article which appeared in a secular counselling magazine a few years ago:

He's 29, he has a good job, his own flat, he is in a stable relationship and he is having a mid-life crisis. 'It crept upon me by stealth,' says Patrick Winston, a publishing executive from Bath. 'I had a great job, a partner, a good social life—everything I'd wanted, but gradually this sense of *ennui* took over and it left me feeling blank and demotivated. I started to feel that my life—including me—was fraudulent. I kept thinking: what next? I went through a period of heavy promiscuity, which made things worse. I felt that all that was in front of me was the same-acquisition of wealth and status, which had come to mean nothing to me. I became impotent, started drinking heavily and hated myself.'

The article went on to point out that the mid-life crisis is creeping downward and hitting younger people. The writer concludes: 'We are living harder, and burning out sooner. The world is dogged by short-termism, in relationships, in work—and this accelerates the process of disenchantment.' Does that ring any bells with you? It certainly would with the Teacher.

But is this *all* there is? This leads us to the third key phrase in (Ecclesiastes 1:3), 'life under the sun'. The Teacher is referring to what we all experience in life from a *purely earthly perspective,* a perspective shared by believer and unbeliever alike; it is the perspective which is the common lot of humanity. There is a dreary, repetitiveness about existence:

The sun rises and the sun sets,
    and hurries back to where it rises.
The wind blows to the south
    and turns to the north;
round and round it goes,
    ever returning to its course.
All streams flow into the sea,
    yet the sea is never full.
To the place the streams come from,
    there they return again.
All things are wearisome
    more than one can say.   (Ecclesiastes 1:5–8)

Things may change on a superficial level; we can split the atom or land a probe on Mars, but pretty well everything remains the same here on earth. There is happiness and misery, love and war, friendships and hatred, work and leisure and then death, which seems to make a mockery of all our achievements. It was the American comedian Woody Allen who said, 'It's not that I am afraid of death, it's just that I don't want to be around when it happens to me.'

In one of his more sober moments he reflected:

> The fundamental thing behind all motivation and all activity is the constant struggle against annihilation and against death. It's absolutely stupefying in its terror, and it renders anyone's accomplishments meaningless. As Camus wrote, it's not only that he the individual dies, or that man as a whole dies, but that you struggle to do a work of art that will last and then you realise that the universe itself is not going to exist after a period of time.[23]

This is something which really does begin to press upon us when there is less ahead than what lies behind because you have hit the 50 mark. That is when you ask, 'Where has the time gone and what have I achieved (what profit have I gained)?'

What is Woody Allen's answer? We create our own fake meaning:

> The universe is indifferent ... so we create a fake world for ourselves, and we exist within that fake world ... a world that, in fact, means nothing at all, when you step back. It's

meaningless. But it's important that we create some sense of meaning, because no perceptible meaning exists for anybody.[24]

Referring to the task of the Teacher, John Walton and Andrew Hill write:

The quest concerns whether there is meaning to be found in life 'under the sun,' or as we would say, 'in this life.' The answer is that each pursuit investigated (wisdom, pleasure, power, legacy) has several potential drawbacks: (1) it proves an unworthy pursuit; (2) it is unachievable (i.e. no matter how much of it you get, there is always more to get); or (3) in the end you die anyway, so what is the point? The author therefore adopts the radical conclusion that there is no sense of self-fulfilment that can bring meaning to life, so the best is to stop pursuing self-fulfilment.[25]

It would be a mistake, however, if we simply viewed the writer as an early day 'Victor Meldrew', located at the nihilistic end of the spectrum of life.[26] Robert K. Johnston gets the balance about right when he says, 'Observable life lacks coherence, and yet the joys of common grace are also to be valued. We will all die, yet God gives us the days of our lives, the ability to eat and find enjoyment, our wealth and work, even our very spirit or breath. Qoheleth challenges readers to hold on to these two realities—*hebel* (vanity) and *simchah* (joy)muting neither.'[27]

The poem
In order to back up this claim that life while fundamentally

good appears fleeting and elusive—*hebel*—full of hard work,
the Teacher presents us with a poem:

> Generations come and generations go,
>   but the earth remains forever.
> The sun rises and the sun sets
>   and hurries back to where it rises.
> The wind blows to the south and
>   turns to the north;
> round and round it goes,
>   ever returning on its course.
> All streams flow into the sea,
>   yet the sea is never full.
> To the place the streams come from,
>   there they return again.
> All things are wearisome,
>   more than one can say.
> The eye never has enough of seeing,
>   nor the ear its fill of hearing.
> What has been will be again,
>   what has been done will be done again;
> there is nothing new under the sun.
> Is there anything of which one can say,
>   'Look! This is something new'?
> It was here already, long ago;
>   it was here before our time.
> There is no remembrance of men of old,
>   And even those who are yet to come
> will not be remembered
>   by those who follow.[28]   (Ecclesiastes 1:4–11)

The writer is saying that while people come and go the world continues as 'the same old same old'. He portrays the elements like the sun and the wind and the seas finding things to be a slog. And to top it all, we as individuals appear on the scene and are but a blink of an eye in the grand scheme of things.

> The worst of it is death. Jog and lift weights until you are eighty-five; aspire to be the healthiest ninety year old in history, but eventually you will be a corpse. Delay the inevitable with skin creams and makeup; keep fit by dieting and exercise; maintain youthful appearance with plastic surgery and liposuction, but eventually your beauty will fade, and if it doesn't fade while you are alive, it will fade when you die. Build a billion-dollar business, spread your product over the globe, effect a massive change in fashion, but eventually your product and your company will grow old and fade away. But that won't bother you, because long before your company dies, you will. Organise and schmooze and network your way to the heights of political power, but soon enough your power will drift away, and if it's not gone before you die it will be gone when you die. Build a tower that reaches to the sky, but someday it will be dust; and if it stands no one will remember your name. If, by some slim chance of fate, your name is remembered, you won't be around to enjoy the acclaim. Write a best-selling book, but when you die the book will have to get along in the world without your help. And you will die. You will end like the stinking bones and skulls at the graveside of Ophelia, quite chop-fallen. Death is for Solomon the great vaporiser.[29]

Similarly, Peter Enns comments on this passage,

The cycle of life, as illustrated even in nature itself, assures that there is no pay off for any of our activities and efforts. All that we do in any corner of our existence collapses to absurdity. Moreover, the ultimate indication of absurdity is the fact that we will all die, and even the hope of being remembered by our descendants is an empty one.[30]

This is what many playwrights of the 20th century have concluded, men like Samuel Beckett and his one minute play, interestingly called, 'Breath.' The curtains open to reveal a stage in total darkness, then we hear the sound of a man's breath, which is like a death rattle and a light comes on to reveal a pile of rubbish, then the lights go out. That is life as far as he is concerned, fleeting, pointless and meaningless.

But is this the *only* perspective, a universe 'without windows'? If so, then mankind is the greatest tragedy in the cosmos, lower than the slugs who are not troubled with thoughts of purpose and significance, they are just getting on with the business of producing slimy trails and doing other slug-like things.

The perspective

However, there *is* another perspective according to Qoheleth which is captured by the slightly different phrase, 'under heaven'. We first come across the term in Ecclesiastes 1:13, 'I devoted myself to study and to explore by wisdom all that is done *under heaven.* What a heavy burden *God* has laid on men!' In Ecclesiastes 5:2 the connection between God and heaven is underscored even more strongly, 'God is in heaven and you are on earth.' It seems that this is a phrase associated with God and his sovereign rule over the world and our lives. It is this perspective which makes all the difference. The phrase associates with the idea that God is carefully superintending his world which is why the rising and setting of the sun is as predictable as it is. The routine nature of things is not all bad; it provides us with a sense of security and assurance, indeed, it is this belief which makes modern science possible.[31] What is more, even the sense of frustration and deep longing we have has been laid upon us by God, so that we might feel unsettled and seek after him by asking the big questions, 'Why are we here? What is the purpose of life?'

Immanuel Kant, the great Enlightenment philosopher, summed up the four big questions of life as 'What can we know? What must we do? What can we hope for? What is man?' 'Meaning is not a luxury for us' writes the Christian philosopher Dallas Willard. 'It is a kind of spiritual oxygen, we might say, that enables our souls to live.'[32]

According to the Teacher the reason why we crave meaning like a man might crave oxygen is because God has placed 'eternity in our hearts' (Ecclesiastes 3:11). In other words, feeling like strangers in a strange land reminds us that our world is a fallen world, dislocated because of our sin; and so it is appropriate that things don't always work out the way we want them to. It is no bad thing that we feel the friction and tensions of life, recognising our world to be a mixture of the 'good, the bad and the ugly', all coming under God's sovereign sway. Isn't it often the case that when things are going along swimmingly, we give little thought to our Maker? However, when things are thrown out of whack, perhaps as we face tragedy and disappointment, and especially death, that's when we become less settled with our superficial plastic way of living and want a taste of reality—true reality which is

God himself. It is when we come to know him as our rightful, loving and wise ruler, who doesn't always explain himself to us (because he doesn't have to, Ecclesiastes 5:5) that we can start to journey through life with a sense of purpose.[33] It is a purpose shaped by knowing, loving and serving the One who made us and enjoying the things of life as gifts with gratitude to the Giver. This is the conclusion reached at the end of the book: 'Now all has been heard; here is the conclusion of the matter: Fear God and keep his commandments, for this is the whole duty of man.' There is therefore an alternative to self-fulfilment, 'the pursuit of a God-centred life. Even though pursuits under the sun may not be capable of providing self-fulfilment or give meaning to life there is much in life that can be enjoyed as the gift of God.'[34]

In short, the Teacher of Ecclesiastes is concerned with enabling people to have right *expectations* about life. If we expect most of life to be plain sailing, with next to no knocks, frustrations or pain, then we are going to be seriously disappointed. If we expect government, work, education or even religion to solve most, if not all, of our problems, then we are going to feel very let down indeed. This is life 'under the sun', an amalgam of joys and sorrows, achievements and failures, satisfaction and frustration. It is a messy world. But when we begin to see God at the centre, life 'under heaven'—recognising that this is still God's good world, full of gifts to enjoy, yet also a world shot through with tragedy and pain—then we can learn something which many of our contemporaries are ignorant of and that is contentment. This is not a Stoic resignation before the world, it is a life which will still involve struggles and questions (often directed at

God), but it will do so in the knowledge of God's eternity and the limits he has set.

If you want honest answers to honest questions then ask them with the Teacher as your guide. But make no mistake, like life itself, it will be a roller coaster of a ride with its emotional highs and lows; there will be plenty of blind alleys too and in addition more well trod paths; dark moments and patches of 'Godlight'. One thing is for sure, the journey will not be a dull one.

Questions for further thought and discussion

How would you answer Tolstoy's questions—what will come of what I do today or tomorrow? What will come of my entire life?

Do you view God and the Bible any differently because it contains Ecclesiastes? To your mind, is Ecclesiastes 'un-Christian'?

In what ways have you or those around you experienced the *hebel*—vanity of life?

What questions about our world and lives do you want to ask at the beginning of the journey with the teacher?

2

Good but not good enough— education, pleasure and work

Ecclesiastes 1:12–2:26

Here is a 'nihilistic soundbite' from taxi driver, Jose Martinez:

> We're here to die, just live and die. I live driving a cab. I do some fishing, take my girl out, pay taxes, do a little reading, then get ready to drop dead. You've got to be strong about it. Life is a big fake. Nobody gives a damn. You're rich or you're poor. You're here, you're gone. You're like the wind. After you're gone, other people will come. It's too late to make it better. Everyone's fed up, can't believe in nothing no more. People have no pride. People have no fear. People aren't scared. People only care about one thing and that's money. We're gonna destroy ourselves, nothing we can do about it. The only cure for the world's illness is nuclear war—wipe everything out

and start over. We've become like a cornered animal, fighting for survival. Life is nothing.[35]

Can you imagine an early morning conversation with him as he takes you down to the railway station to catch your train! But that is what he thinks, as do millions of others like him. This man has probably never heard of Ecclesiastes let alone read it, and yet we find him echoing all too clearly much of what the Teacher wrote thousands of years ago. He also is of the view that we are 'like the wind'.

As we have seen, our author is a King, and what today would be called a believer. Being true to his faith in the God of Israel he is also a man of integrity, an honest man who wants to ask honest questions and receive honest answers. The big question which undergirds all his other questions is: 'Is there a lasting benefit from life "under the sun"?' That is, what can we really expect from life as we know it? The reality is that many of the things we experience, are, as he puts in 1:14, 'meaningless', (Hebrew: *hebel*); like bubbles or smoke, elusive and transitory. This is the situation in which you think you are on to a winner but what you were putting you hope in disappears before your very eyes. The result is that life is experienced as a 'chasing after the wind', a futile enterprise. The feeling we have that life is meant to be so much more and yet never within our grasp is actually God-given, according to 1:13, 'What a heavy burden God has laid on men.' It is like spots which irritate our skin but which are symptoms of a deeper, underlying disease which needs dealing with, in this case, estrangement from God. The Bible tells us that we live 'East of Eden', out of sorts with our Maker and consequently out of kilter with his world and each other. In short, we are constantly being reminded by our disappointments, frustrations and longings, that we need rescuing from the human predicament. This is why God in his sovereign power and gracious love has put eternity into our hearts (3:11). We are not just reproductive biological machines, or plastic people whose lives are built on pleasure and entertainment, we are spiritual beings designed to have a personal relationship with our Maker. Therefore, trying to find ultimate satisfaction in anything else is doomed to failure, as we shall see.

However, the Teacher does not adopt what was later to become known as the 'Aristotelian' approach to knowledge, remotely sitting in some ivory tower theorising about the world. He adopts what is more akin to a 'scientific stance'; he wants to get first hand experience of things by engaging in empirical observation to see what he can come up with: 'I thought to myself, "Look, I have grown and increased in wisdom more than anyone who has ruled over Jerusalem before me; I have experienced much of wisdom and knowledge."' (2:16) More specifically he launches himself into looking at three areas of life which might offer some kind of hope that substantial value and purpose might be found—what we can conveniently describe as *probing, pleasure* and *projects.*

Probing

First of all, *probing,* that is, the pursuit of knowledge and wisdom or, as we might say, education (1:16–18; 2:12–16). From the middle of the 19th century throughout the 20th century and into our own, education has been seen to be the great hope for mankind. With better education we will have a more civilised society—so it was thought. Two World Wars and umpteen minor conflicts later have not seen that belief diminishing. Personally, I believe having a good education is one of the greatest blessings we can have, it transforms lives; it certainly has mine. But is it really the case that gaining more knowledge in itself produces the better life, the good life? Not necessarily according to the Qoheleth

> Then I applied myself to the understanding of wisdom, and also of madness and folly, but I learned that this, too, is a chasing after the wind. For with much wisdom comes much sorrow; the more knowledge, the more grief. (1:17)

What does he mean? He could be referring to the experience that the more we know, the more we realize how much we don't know! This is well captured by the little 'mental knot' of R. D. Laing: 'If I don't know I don't know I think I know. If I don't know I know I think I don't know.' We can never get to the bottom of the well of wisdom; it just goes down deeper and deeper. It can be quite frustrating to come to the point when you realise that there is so little you do know after all the hard study, exams and self-sacrifice. Education is good thing, but not a lasting thing. Isn't it strange how quickly those things which seemed so important at the time begin to fade? You may recall all the hard work for those GCSEs or 'A' levels or a degree, remembering how you felt once those grades were posted on the college notice board. It was terrific (if you achieved the grades you wanted that is). But how do you feel about them now? Not that much I would guess. Good things which are not lasting things.

In the second place, increased knowledge brings with it

an increased awareness of misery which in turn makes us miserable and frustrated as we realise how so little can be done in the face of the huge problems and challenges before us. This doesn't mean we simply sit back and don't try to do anything, rather it puts a check on any dewy-eyed idealism we once may have had that the world will invariably get better mainly through learning. Let me give a personal example. Many might think it a wonderful opportunity to travel to South Africa, as I have done, in order to gain knowledge. This is true in some ways, but not in others. I think, for instance, of my experience at a place called Lavender Hill. What a wonderful name for a town. It sounds so idyllic. It is in fact a run-down Black Township on the edge of Cape Town. It is a scene of abject poverty, the likes of which many people living in Britain could not even begin to imagine. It is also a place of the most unspeakable evil. Armed gangs frequently engage in gun battles in the open streets with folk getting killed in the cross-fire. Unimaginable things are done to little children, including babies, on a daily basis in the form of sexual abuse. The week before I arrived a policeman had been shot dead just around the corner from the church in broad daylight. A decapitated body was once found lying on the church steps at which I was ministering. A number of years ago, after a Christian instruction class, four young girls set off from the church only to be raped in full view of a watching crowd in the middle of the street. When the minister tried to intervene, he was told leave well alone or he would be killed. What do you do with that kind of knowledge? It makes you feel quite sick and dispirited. 'With much wisdom comes much sorrow'.

This is not to say there really is no difference between living a wise life and living foolishly: 'I saw that wisdom is better than folly, just as light is better than darkness. The wise man has eyes in his head, while the fool walks in the darkness.' (2:13). In terms of general physical and mental health and quality of relationships, there are tremendous advantages in living a sensible life, using our minds and getting enjoyment out of learning. The Teacher is not denying those things for a moment. This is one of the reasons why Christians have often been found to be at the vanguard of education in the West, it is part of expressing our God given image; we have minds which are to be used for God's glory. But if this life is *all there is*, life 'under the sun', then what is the point of cramming your head with more and more knowledge when you are going to be occupying a grave next to someone who just didn't even bother?

> Then I thought in my heart, 'The fate of the fool will overtake me also. What then do I gain by being wise?' 'This too is meaningless.' For the wise man, like the fool, will not be long remembered; in days to come both will be forgotten. Like the fool, the wise man too must die! (2:15)

If you excel in your academic achievements, there may be some bronze bust made of you which is perched on a shelf at a red-brick university somewhere, but what value is that when death levels everybody out, such that the prodigal and the professor both end up as worm food? We are back to everything being *hebel*—mist and vapour, elusive and transitory!

The very nature of education takes us to the heart of the 'big questions' about life in general as mentioned in chapter

1. This was something T. S. Eliot drew attention to in his lecture, 'The Aims of Education', delivered to the University of Chicago in 1951:

> But the moment we ask about the purpose of anything, we may be involving ourselves in asking about the purpose of everything. If we define education, we are led to ask 'What is Man?', and if we define the purpose of education, we are committed to the question 'What is Man for?' Every definition of the purpose of education, therefore, implies some concealed or rather implicit philosophy or theology.[36]

This has important implications regarding both the limits of education and its basis. A purely secular viewpoint, which admits of no God, no transcendent values, has no alternative but to attempt to answer the big questions solely from the 'inside', which will almost inevitably result in some form of reductionism: man being nothing more than a 'naked ape' or the like. But for someone who believes that there is a God, then there is a possibility of answers being given from the 'outside', from God himself which enables us to have a sense of value and purpose.

The writer Harry Blamires notes the fundamental difference in these terms:

> Surely the Christian is distinguished from the secularist, roughly speaking, by having a double allegiance—to this life which he shares with the secularist and to another life into which his faith admits him ... In bringing Christian thinking to bear upon anything, we regard it in its two aspects, in nature and under God. This applies to the simplest and most complex

of things in life; simple things like daily meals for instance. The secularist sees food as the product of the earth and of man's labour. The Christian sees it as that and also as the gift of God—and gives thanks accordingly.[37]

The 'cash value' of the difference would be seen on the ground in the way a Christian teacher would approach matters:

> The Christian teacher will apply this double vision both to his pupils and to his subject. He will learn to look at his pupils not only as children of men but as children of God—fellow beings with souls to save. He will learn to look at the subject he teaches not only as part of the fabric of human knowledge, but also as related to those truths of Christian revelation which sum up our knowledge of life and its meaning.[38]

The secularist is locked into a world where there is nothing but 'life under the sun'—cold and dark.

> For the secularist, this world of breathing and eating, calculating and measuring, getting and spending, flourishing and fading, aging and dying, is the total sum of things. The secularist, talk of 'purpose' or 'meaning,' 'end' or 'cause' related to what has been done on this planet or what can be done on this planet by the planet's own natural products, manipulating its resources with their five senses and their five wits within the straitjacketing dimension called 'time.' For the materialist there is nothing else.[39]

However, for the Teacher, and others who believe in a

Creator-Redeemer God, there is 'life under heaven' and depending upon where one stands in relation to these two positions, a 'culture clash' is inevitable for there are radically different perceptions of reality and value. For the thorough-going secularist, life will be seen as a matter of progress from cradle to the grave with personal well-being the primary concern. The Christian, however, would see people as heading towards eternity, souls of infinite value needing saving, a fellow traveller for whom God came into the world, becoming one of them in order to die to rescue them. These two visions are fundamentally at odds with each other and cannot be papered over.[40] Learning too is a chasing after the wind.

Pleasure

But even within the Biblical framework and the immense goods provided as a result, education cannot provide deep satisfaction nor deliver 'the bottom line'. It is not surprising, therefore, that people turn to the pursuit of pleasure in an attempt to fill the 'god shaped gap' spoken of by Blaise Pascal, or as the author of Ecclesiastes puts it:

> I thought in my heart, 'Come now, I will test you with pleasure to find out what is good.' But that also proved to be meaningless. 'Laughter,' I said, 'is foolish. And what does pleasure accomplish?' I tried cheering myself with wine, and embracing folly—my mind still guiding me with wisdom. I wanted to see what was worthwhile for men to do under heaven during the few days of their lives. (2:1–3)

Today this would be seen as the ever popular route of

consumerism, whatever will make us feel good we purchase. It is the mentality of 'shop until your drop.' Somehow we have to inject into ourselves the high octane fuel of enjoyment which will produce the necessary 'lift' to help us cope with what is otherwise a mundane existence. Again, let us not misunderstand our writer. As we shall see towards the end of this chapter, having pleasure and enjoyment are good things but they can never become *the* thing; that which motivates us to get out of bed in the morning in order to live productive, meaningful lives.

To begin with, pleasure can never be sought in and of itself, it is always a *by-product* of something else. For instance, you gain a profound sense of delight in having a conversation with a friend—it is so rich you don't realize you have been talking for three hours when it has only seemed like three minutes. The activity is the *conversation* of friends and the pleasure gained is the by-product. And so one could go on and think of the pleasures of reading, listening to music, going to the cinema, sex—these are all activities which can lead to pleasure, but to try and base our lives *solely* on pleasure seeking is like chasing after the wind, it can't be done. Certainly the advertisers will tell us differently, but it is a lie. We are left feeling empty, craving more, which of course, is what the advertisers want.

Happiness has proved elusive in the contemporary world. By any conceivable measure of the good life, we are better off than any previous generation since the birth of time. We are more affluent. We have more choices. We can travel further and more easily. We have more access to education and information. Our health is better. We live longer. We keep ourselves fit. We have leisure. We are freer. There are fewer constraints on our lifestyles. We are living, compared to any previous generation, as close to paradise as people have ever lived. Yet by the indexes of self-reported life satisfaction, we are no happier than people were two generations ago. In some respects our lack of happiness is palpable. We take more anti-depressants. People suffer from more stress-related syndromes. They are less optimistic than they used to be. They no longer think their children will have better lives than they did. There has been a palpable breakdown of trust.[41]

Of course, in our narcissistic culture many derive pleasure and seek significance from what we eat, drink and wear. 'Eat, drink and be merry for tomorrow we diet' is the modern twist on an ancient Greek adage, and the Teacher himself certainly seemed to enjoy the drink side of things (2:2). This drive for significance through possession and image has been given an almost irresistible momentum through the power of advertising. 'Advertising' says the cynic 'is the art of getting people to buy what they don't need by describing it in ways they know are not true.' In the West, advertising is more than big business it is a way of life, for what is most commonly associated with advertising is now the very thing which shapes the way many people look and behave, namely, *style.* What is style—but *self*-advertising.[42] To choose a certain style is to choose a certain image we want to project to the world. And so, *identity*—who we are—merges into *image*—what we want to appear to be. So the old adage 'You are what you eat' (which is attributed to the philosopher Nietzsche) has been transmuted into 'You are what you wear.' The whole fashion industry is totally dependent upon us believing this.

It is the fashion industry in particular which both expresses and enforces the Teacher's dictum that life is mist—*hebel*—a chasing after the wind, for is there anything more transitory than fashion? The ever-changing, non-permanence of style is the hallmark of postmodernity:

> Postmodern society is a rush and roil of change, and our selves get caught up in the whirl. Nothing stays fixed; every new thing flows into something else before it can harden into habit. The style industry exists to keep producing new styles, to keep everyone thinking that they have to buy a new wardrobe each year to keep up, to bring shame to everyone uncool enough to wear last season's colours … A celebrity, Daniel Boorstin has said, is someone well known for being well known. But the half time of fame is extremely short, and to keep yourself in the public eye and keep ahead of the game you have to be willing to make yourself over again and again.[43]

If ever there was a chasing after the wind it is seeking to find significance and worth through style.

Projects

If the unbridled pursuit of pleasure proves to be a dead end, what else might be explored? Why not immerse yourself in projects, working at something you hope will last?

> I undertook great projects: I built houses for myself and planted vineyards. I made gardens and parks and planted all kinds of fruit trees in them. I made reservoirs to water groves of flourishing trees. I bought male and female slaves and had other slaves who were born in my house. I also owned

more herds and flocks than anyone in Jerusalem before me. I
amassed silver and gold for myself, and the treasure of kings
and provinces. I acquired men and women singers, and a
harem as well—the delights of the heart of man. I became
greater by far than anyone in Jerusalem before me. In all this
my wisdom stayed with me. I denied myself nothing my eyes
desired; I refused my heart no pleasure. My heart took delight
in all my work, and this was the reward for all my labour.

(2:4–10)

This man really throws himself into things head first and
with every ounce of energy he has. Of course, he has the
power and the money to do it; he is the king after all, so no
expense is spared. Again, note that there *is* satisfaction in
these things—he says so in verse 10. This is because we are
made in God's image and as God is the great worker and
project maker—bringing a universe into being, in our own
small way we are to be like this too. I love projects, I am not
mad about gardening—I leave that to my wife—but planning
things and bringing them to completion brings a tremendous
amount of satisfaction and sense of achievement. *But*, they
have their limitations: 'Yet when I surveyed all that my hands
had done and what I had toiled to achieve, everything was
meaningless, a chasing after the wind; nothing was gained
under the sun.' (2:11) Why is that?

First, it is *toil* and leads to anxiety, 'All his days his work is
pain and grief; even at night his mind does not rest. This too
is meaningless' (2:23). Here is a candid admission from the
late actor, John Thaw (TV's Inspector Morse):

I suppose I am a workaholic. It's all about needing to work to give yourself some importance, to prove that you exist. If I have a month or two off with nothing happening I get very fidgety, nervy, edgy. It isn't insecurity because I know there's work coming up. It must be, I suppose, that I need work so as to be able to say to people: 'Look, I'm here. I exist.'[44]

A similar sentiment has been expressed by Madonna:

My drive in life comes from a fear of being mediocre. That is always pushing me. I push past one spell of it and discover myself as a special human being but then feel I am still mediocre and uninteresting unless I do something else. Because even though I have become somebody, I still have to prove that I am somebody. My struggle has never ended and I guess it never will.[45]

Perhaps this is an accurate description of you. Could it be that the reason why you are taking that extra educational course, stretching yourself to the limit, at the expense of your family and friends and maybe even your health, is because deep down it is in your work, or gaining that qualification, that you are seeking your identity? Without it you feel like you are nothing or just plain mediocre. You want to be well thought of, which is why you are working all the hours that God gives you. But you are never really satisfied. That is why you have to go on to the next thing, and the next—you are driven. If that is the case, can you see what you are doing? You are making a good thing into *the* thing—in short, an idol.

The second reason the Teacher gives for the folly of working more and more and faster and faster is that you never live to enjoy the full benefits of what you have worked for, it can be left to someone else who comes along later only to squander it all:

> I hated all the things I had toiled for under the sun, because I must leave them to the one who comes after me. And who knows whether he will be a wise man or a fool? Yet he will have control over all the work into which I have poured my effort and skill under the sun. This too is meaningless. So my heart began to despair over all my toilsome labour under the sun.
>
> (2:18–19)

Has this not been the experience of many of the rich and famous, having offspring who, to be honest, couldn't hold a candle to their parents and who just throw it all away? Of course not only the rich and famous—we can all think of examples.

Someone we might have expected to have felt some great satisfaction in all his achievements was the man who invented dynamite—Alfred Nobel. Yet this is how he described himself: 'Alfred Nobel—pitiful creature, ought to have been suffocated by a humane physician when he made his howling entrance into this life ... Important events in this life: none.'

Near his death he wrote: 'How pitiful to strive to be someone or something in the motley crowd of 1.4 billion two-legged tailless apes whining around on our revolving earth projectile.'[46]

'Bubbles, bubbles, everything is a chasing after the wind'. The lesson is clear, if we expect to find lasting satisfaction from what we learn, our pleasures, or projects, then we must be prepared to be disappointed. Get ready to look back on your life with your head in your hands muttering 'What a waste'. Folk living in the United States are keen on car bumper stickers. I wonder what kind of bumper stickers the Teacher would have on his car. Maybe something like, 'Eat well, stay fit, die anyway'; 'He who dies with the most toys, simply dies'; 'Shrouds have no pockets'. All the striving and struggling for more and more things, lead to the graveyard and the landfill site. It all seems so trivial and wasteful.

However, there does appear to be a certain self-centredness in the Teacher's ambitions. As Jonathan Sacks observes,

> Nowhere in the Old Testament is the first person singular (*I*), used so relentlessly and repetitively. In the original Hebrew the effect is doubled because of the chiming of the verbal suffix and the pronoun: *Baniti li, asiti li, kaniti li*, 'I build for myself, I made for myself, I bought for myself.' The source of the Teacher's unhappiness is obvious and was spelled out many centuries later by the great sage Hillel: 'If I am not for myself, who will I be? But if I am only for myself, what am I?'[47]

This underscores the point made earlier that one can never find satisfaction in pleasure by seeking pleasure, it is a by product of something else—especially relationships. Happiness in the Bible is not something we find in self-gratification. Hence, the significance of the Hebrew word *simchah*. It can be translated as 'joy', but really it has no precise translation into English, since all our words expressing emotion refer to states of mind we can experience alone. *Simchah* is something we cannot experience alone: *simchah* is joy shared.[48]

Does this mean that there is no ray of sunshine amidst all

the doom and gloom? Is there any good news-gospel? Yes
there is—sort of:

> A man can do nothing better than to eat and drink and
> find satisfaction in his work. This too, I see, is from the hand
> of God, for without him, who can eat or find enjoyment? To
> the man who pleases him, God gives wisdom, knowledge and
> happiness, but to the sinner he gives the task of gathering and
> storing up wealth to hand it over to the one who pleases God.
> This too is meaningless, a chasing after the wind.   (2:24–26)

There are many things in life which we can and should
enjoy—food, company, work, family, friendship—the list is
almost endless. There is genuine satisfaction in these things,
but there is an altogether richer satisfaction when we see
them for what they truly are—*gifts from God*. The value of
these things does not simply reside in themselves but as they
lead us to the one who gives them—God. Then they are not
just items floating around meaninglessly in a disconnected
fashion on a sea of endless activity, they are emblems of
grace, God's loving kindness. This makes all the difference
in the world to the way we view and experience life. The
writer G. K. Chesterton said that the 'chief idea of my life' is
the practice of 'taking things with gratitude and not taking
things for granted.' He would have agreed with the artist
Dante Gabriel Rossetti, 'The worst moment for an atheist is
when he is genuinely thankful but has nobody to thank.'[49]
Seeing food, drink and work as gifts totally transforms our
view of the universe for everything is conceived in personal
terms. Instead of work being nothing but a drag, it becomes
a vocation, a calling. Instead of food being the result of

some meaningless biological system, it is viewed as a kindly gift from a heavenly Father. The whole of creation becomes infused with a new wonder and delight where everything is seen as a gift to be received with gratitude. What a difference it makes to my little granddaughter, Chloe, for example, when I take her by the hand to the shop and buy her something which together we can play with and talk about, instead of it just appearing in her room one day without any note of explanation. She is thrilled and excited about it and so am I. It is meant to be like that between ourselves and God.

At the Graduation Address of Harvard University in 1978, Alexander Solzhenitsyn addressed his distinguished audience with these words:

> If humanism were right in declaring that man is born to be happy, he would not be born to die. Since his body is doomed to die his task on earth … must be of a more spiritual nature. It cannot be the unrestrained enjoyment of everyday life. It cannot be the search for the best way to obtain material goods and then cheerfully to get the most out of them. It has to be the fulfilment of a permanent earnest duty so that one's life journey may become an experience of moral growth, so that one may leave life a better human being than when one started it.

Solzhenitsyn *had* read Ecclesiastes and what is more, believed it. But notice what Solzhenitsyn assumes: he presupposes that this life is not the only one, otherwise being a better human being at the end is also futile for you die like all the others who were not better human beings. There *must* be eternity. It is that perspective, living *under* heaven and then *in* heaven which transforms this life, where God through

Christ becomes our Father. This life *is* a breath, a bubble, but the next life is shared with God who is eternal and it is the security of knowing that is where we are heading which makes this life worth while.

Questions for further thought and discussion

Think about the pursuit of our three categories in this chapter—Probing (education), pleasure and projects.

For each one, ask these questions:

How do you personally 'chase after' this?

What are you hoping it will deliver you in life? (e.g. a good education = a good job and financial security)

In what ways does it succeed and in what ways does it fail to deliver?

How does knowing God transform how we pursue this part of life?

G. K. Chesterton advises 'taking things with gratitude and not taking things for granted.' Spend some time in thanks to God for what he has given you in education, pleasure and projects.

3

The animal that asks

Ecclesiastes 3

Walter Lippmann was one of the most influential American political commentators of the 20th century. This is what he once wrote about modern Western man:

At ... heart ... there are likely to be moments of blank misgiving in which he finds that the civilization of which he is a part leaves a dusty taste in his mouth, he may be very busy with many things, but he discovers one day that he is no longer sure they are worth doing. He has been much preoccupied: but he is no longer sure he knows why. He has become involved in an elaborate routine of pleasures; and they do not seem to amuse him very much. He finds it hard to believe that doing any one thing is better than doing any other thing, or, in fact, that it is better than doing nothing at all. It occurs to him that it is a great deal of trouble to live, and that even in

the best lives the thrills are few and far between. He begins
more or less consciously to seek satisfactions, because he is no
longer satisfied, and all the while he realises that the pursuit of
happiness was always a most unhappy quest.[50]

This appears to be an astute assessment of the present
scene. The writer of Ecclesiastes would also have said that
it would have been a shrewd analysis of his own day some
3,000 years or so earlier: 'Mist, mist everything is mist—a
chasing after the wind.' In an attempt to discover if there is
a 'bottom line' to life, something which gives significance to
our short stay on earth, time and time again the Teacher is
left with a profound sense of emptiness and frustration. For
while things seem good, with so much to enjoy, he appears to
be suddenly knocked sideways and left wondering with Alfie,
'What's it all about?' And yet, deep down there is a sense that
while we share the same fate as the animals, namely, death
(3:19–20), we are nonetheless more than the animals, we can't
escape the feeling that there is more to life under the sun,
something or Someone who can tie it all together. The literary
critic George Steiner put the matter quite simply, 'More than
Homo sapiens, we are *Homo quarens,* the animal that asks
and asks.'[51] In chapter 3 of his *magnum opus,* the Teacher
comes tantalising close to discovering the answer as to what
that 'something' is; it is not a neat and tidy answer to be sure,
but it is a promising one. The solution to our existence here
on earth is to be found in having a proper appreciation of the
relationship between time and eternity.

A pattern to be discerned

There is a pattern which human beings can discern according

to vv. 1–8. 'There is a time for everything, and a season for every activity (it could be translated 'purpose') under heaven.' (v. 1) The Teacher then goes on to compare and contrast the kinds of things which have their 'season'—birth and death, killing and healing, war and peace, silence and speaking. He is making the claim that there is a universal recognition of the *timeliness* of things. No matter where you go on earth, or which culture you care to look at, in whichever period of history, everyone recognises that there is a pattern to life, a right time to do certain things and a wrong time. The wisdom comes in discerning which is which.

For example, you can have the right thing at the right time, but also the right thing at the wrong time which makes it the wrong thing. Accordingly, says the Teacher, there is 'a time for peace and a time for war'.

Many people will be familiar with the name of David Niven, the English actor who starred in a number of Hollywood blockbuster films like *The Guns of Navarone* and *The Pink Panther*. Niven went to Hollywood in the 1930s and became a close friend of legendary 'hell raiser', Errol Flynn. He had just made his breakthrough as a leading star as *Raffles* in 1939 when war broke out in Europe. Out of a deep sense of duty he, unlike many other English actors in Hollywood, left America for Britain and signed up for the army, eventually attaining the rank of Colonel in the Commandos. Niven lost many close friends during the war and saw many dreadful things happen. On returning to Hollywood in 1945 he was given a welcome party by his actor colleagues. At that event he said that he would only ever speak of the war at that party and would never talk about it again. He went on to say he could never forgive the weak-willed, crass stupidity of the politicians who allowed the war to happen in the first place, resulting in the loss of so many lives and the unleashing of so much misery. As far as he was concerned there *was* a time for war in order to avoid a greater war, and that was when Adolf Hitler marched his troops to re-occupy the Rhineland. Had he been stopped then while he was relatively weak, much of the carnage of the Second World War could have been avoided.[52] Instead, a policy of appeasement encouraged Hitler on with his megalomaniacal ambitions. The right thing—'peace' became the wrong thing—'appeasement' because it was pursued at the wrong time.

What about love and hate?

A case can be made that there was a right time to love Hitler. When he was a baby for example, it would have been right to love him then. When he came out of the army after the First World War as a penniless aspiring artist, humiliated and resentful, wouldn't that have been a good time for someone to love him? But hate would not be too strong a word to describe the appropriate response to Hitler and his followers when you read accounts of the Holocaust such as this:

> The other gas chambers were full of the adults and therefore the children were not gassed, but just burned alive. There were several thousand of them. When one of the SS sort of had pity upon the children, he would take the child and beat the head against a stone before putting it on the pile of fire and wood, so the child lost consciousness. However, the regular way they did it was by just throwing the children onto the pile. They would put a sheet of wood there, then sprinkle the whole thing with petrol, then wood again, and petrol and wood, and petrol—

then they placed the children there. Then the whole thing would be ignited.[53]

There is a time for hate

The point the Teacher is reflecting upon is that everyone has a sense of the timeliness of things in the world. The universe is not random and chaotic. We live in a universe which has all the hallmarks of a cosmos—the well designed, intricate purposeful motions of planets, not the haphazard meanderings of rocks thrown around by Chance.

But what of the 'disorder' in the world which makes some wonder if the world is not as neatly arranged as the Teacher here seems to be suggesting? The Teacher is certainly aware of what philosophers call 'the surd', those elements of life which do appear chaotic and even contradictory: 'It is better to go to a house of mourning than to go to a house of feasting, for death is the destiny of every man; the living should take this to heart. Sorrow is better than laughter, because a sad face is good for the heart.' (7:2–3)

It might be said, however, that the fact that we *know* we live in a world predominantly of order causes us to believe that there exists a God we *can* question when we come across the disorder—especially suffering and death (7:2). After all, if the universe is essentially random and at rock bottom meaningless with no rhyme or reason, we would not be asking the question: Why suffering? It would make no more sense to ask that question than to ask, 'Why dry rot?' It just 'is'.

We may think of the matter like this. Suppose you want to lay a square patio of crazy paving in your garden and so you order a wagon load of broken flagstones. Then you start the tricky business of piecing them together. You will not be surprised in the least to find that when you have finished you are left with some pieces that can't be placed anywhere. You are not surprised because you never thought that random, broken pieces were *designed* to fill up your square. You would certainly not think of ringing up your supplier in order to complain that he didn't send the right type of flagstones!

But suppose you buy a jigsaw puzzle from a shop. You fit it all together carefully and thoughtfully, but at the end you are left with gaps and some pieces which don't even belong to the puzzle. *Now* you do have a right to be miffed and ring up to complain to the manufacturers. Why? Because underlying your complaint is the belief (rightly so) that there is an intention, purpose and design behind the jigsaw puzzle. It is precisely the matter of design which makes a jigsaw different from crazy paving.

And so it is with suffering. Suffering, we feel, doesn't quite fit in to the scheme of things. There would be no cause for complaint if underneath it all we didn't believe that the world *was* consciously designed by a good God. So, paradoxical though it may seem, the fact that we feel we have a right to complain is *evidence* that we really do believe there is a God to complain to, believing that our world is more like a well designed jigsaw puzzle with some pieces missing rather than a pile of crazy paving we are expected to put together somehow.

The questions begging to be answered are these: Where did this pattern come from? Why is it that we live in a cosmos and not a chaos? Why is it that there is a *uni*verse rather than a *multi*verse?

Of course the secularist and atheist can only reply that

'under the sun' there is no real pattern or purpose. It just *seems* that there is a pattern which suggests a purpose. But this is nothing more than an illusion, a cosmic con-trick, for at rock bottom the universe is cold, meaningless and without rhyme or reason—so says the likes of Richard Dawkins and the late Christopher Hitchens. But even to speak of a 'cosmic con trick' suggests intention and purpose—the aim of deluding someone. If this is so, then the conclusion in chapter 3:9 is the only one we can come to, 'What does the worker gain from his toil?' What is the bottom line? The answer is that there isn't one—it is all going to pass away and we with it *if* this world is all that there is. But it does raise some basic questions. Why does life appear to have a pattern and purpose if, in fact, it doesn't? Where do we get our sense of right and wrong from? Could it not be that there *is* something in the pattern of the seasons? Perhaps they are pointers to something beyond this world, to an existence which is more than 'life under the sun', indicating that there is 'life under *heaven*'—a spiritual dimension.

A God to be revered

This leads on to the Teacher's next meditation vv. 10–15.

> I have seen the burden God has laid on men. He has made everything beautiful in its time. He has also set eternity in the hearts of men; yet they cannot fathom what God has done from beginning to end. I know that there is nothing better for men than to be happy and do good while they live. That everyone may eat and drink, and find satisfaction in all his toil—this is the gift of God. I know that everything God does will endure

forever; nothing can be added to it and nothing taken from it. God does it so that men will revere him.

The sense that there is more to life than what we can see, hear and touch is a gift of God says our writer, although it feels to us like a burden for reasons we shall see in a moment. It is *God* who 'has made everything beautiful in its time'.

Belief in God or gods is a universal phenomenon, spanning every culture in every age. Atheism is a minority belief; it always has been and, in all likelihood, always will be. People should not be browbeaten into thinking that it is the atheists who are the only intelligent and brave people who are willing to look life squarely in the eyes and say that it is bleak and meaningless, such that the majority of mankind have got it wrong and only they have got it right. Why should they? They *might* have a case if the vast majority of things that happened were chaotic and ugly, but then they would have an additional problem in using reason to come to their conclusions, because reason is orderly and, in a sense, beautiful, so where did that come from—the ability to declare that everything is random and meaningless with the exception of their reason which is ordered and meaningful? No, the irony is that even their ability to use reason to try and disprove God's existence is given to them by God and is one of the best indicators that there is a God.

Some atheists have been more honest regarding their motivation in seeking to discount the existence of God, like Aldous Huxley, and it has very little to do with reason.

In a moment of great candour he confessed,

For myself, no doubt, as for many of my contemporaries, the philosophy of meaninglessness was essentially liberation from a certain political and economic system and liberation from a certain system of morality. We objected to the morality because it interfered with our sexual freedom; we objected to the political and economic system because it was unjust. The supporters of these systems claimed that in some way they embodied the meaning (a Christian meaning they insisted) of the world. There was one admirably simple method of confuting these people and at the same time justifying ourselves in our political and erotic revolt: We could deny that the world had any meaning whatsoever.[54]

The path of atheism is bleak as Leszek Kołakowski saw with such startling clarity:

The absence of God, when consistently upheld and thoroughly examined, spells the ruin of man in the sense that it demolishes or robs of meaning everything we have been used to think of as the essence of being human: the quest for truth, the distinction of good and evil, the claim to dignity, the claim to creating something that withstands the indifferent destructiveness of time.[55]

But here the writer of Ecclesiastes, with the majority of humanity, says that what we see, together with our sense of morality and purpose, act, in the words of the sociologist Peter Berger, as 'signals of transcendence'.[56] Just as you may pick up a weak signal on your car radio which indicates that someone is transmitting a programme and you try and tune in to achieve clarity, so the creation itself, together with life and all its joys and blessings which we are meant to delight in—vv. 12–13, are meant to provoke us to follow the signal to their source, namely, God. This, in part, is what is meant by that key phrase in verse 11, 'He has also set eternity in the hearts of men.' We know there is something bigger than us, something which should make sense of our day-to-day existence, the growing realisation that there is eternity as well as time, a heaven as well as earth.

Robert Johnston summarises the Teacher's view of God and the universe well when he writes:

> Qoheleth's understanding of God … reveals the same paradox as does his understanding of life. God is present yet absent. He gives meaning to life yet it is incomprehensible. He makes both the beautiful and the burdensome. Believers, whether Jewish or Christian, have questioned for centuries why God's gracious personal presence is not more evident in Qoheleth's text. But such is sometimes the reality of life. We too sometimes cry out for God's presence, given his absence. Given external circumstances that cause us to question life, we can either harden our hearts or look for faint motions of grace. Qoheleth chooses the latter—one's food and drink, one's companions and work—to uncover the presence of God's Spirit. He finds God's footprints to be present, even in life's darkest moments. Neither death nor life's amorality nor life's ongoing mystery can cancel out his belief in God's sustaining presence. They in fact, somehow compel it.[57]

At the funeral of his own father, management consultant Charles Handy suddenly realized how this modest man had affected the lives of hundreds in ways he could never have imagined. He then went on to say,

> I realized that what one believes about life and the point of life does matter. I had put my faith, until that moment, in success, money and family, probably in that order. I still think these things are important, although I would now reverse the order, *but I hanker after a bigger frame in which to put them.*[58]

That's the point; we need some bigger picture of life in which to place our little lives for things to make sense. Like Charles Handy, that is what we 'hanker' for.

It is at this juncture, however, that we encounter the problem and the burden, namely—we can't access that bigger picture. This is underscored in the latter part of v. 11, '... *yet they cannot fathom what God has done from beginning to end.*' Deep down we know there is more to life than this; we may have an innate awareness that there is a Maker of it all (what the theologian John Calvin called the *sensus divinitatis*—a sense of the divine), but we can't connect with him and neither can we fathom what his purpose is. The result is that we feel frustrated. It is in our frustration that we turn to making idols, creating things to try to give us purpose, including religions with our own ideas of a god which we can control. But they are all made up and so can never satisfy us and give us the answers we crave—why should they if we have simply constructed them? Of course, a lot of people simply try to avoid thinking about it altogether. In the words of psychologist Ernest Becker, 'Modern man is drinking and drugging himself out of awareness or he spends his time shopping, which is the same thing.' In short: we distract ourselves.

The question remains: why has God put us in this seemingly impossible position of seeing patterns in life but never knowing the purpose, of being aware that there is right and wrong but being unable to find a sufficient basis for them? The answer is given in verse 14, 'God does it so that men will revere him or "fear" him.' That is, when we are faced with the big questions of life, 'Who am I?', 'Why are we here?' we are *meant* to feel hopeless and helpless. We are to sense that there is a God and he is very, very great and we are very, very small. This is the God who without having to engage in the kind of thinking process we have to engage in when we are making things—planning that if we do this then we also have to do that—instantaneously and timelessly God knows *all* things. He just knows and wills into existence the atoms and the galaxies; he just 'knows' all the biochemical processes which enable us to live; he simply 'knows' the exact detail of every baby born into this world and every decision they will ever make and a zillion and one other things which make up this complex and amazing universe in which we find ourselves. He doesn't have to work any of these things out like we do in terms of premises and conclusions—his knowledge is complete and inexhaustible. This is what the word 'omniscience' means.

Realising this, we are meant to be humbled before such a God and moved to worship him. As the beauty of a crimson sunset is savoured, as an exquisite piece of music is delighted in, as you hold that little miracle—your baby son or daughter in your arms—you are meant to exclaim, 'What God can do all of this? What do I know in comparison?' In other words, we should be humbled to such an extent that we say: 'This is such an awesome, glorious, intricate and complex universe of such vastness and yet with so many blessings coming my way, millions of them on a daily basis—what kind of God is it who creates it and keeps it all going?'—v. 15. The greatness of it all and the frustration of it all are intended to bring us to the point where we cry out, 'I don't know you God! I don't know what you are doing or why am I here. Please help me!'

A judgement to face

There is one more thing in this chapter which causes our writer, and maybe ourselves, a certain amount of perplexity and concern, and that is the matter of injustice—vv. 16–22.

> And I saw something else under the sun: In the place of judgement—wickedness was there, in the place of justice—wickedness was there.

This is the great stumbling block to many, the question: where is ultimate justice to be found?

A number of years ago in Nottingham, a judge sentenced a family to prison after hearing how the children, some of them in nappies, had been pulled from their beds and sexually assaulted at sex parties. The judge told the two mothers, 'You must have sat there when these parties were going on and heard your children screaming and did nothing about it.' Are we to say that such things are wrong and not simply distasteful? What about the terrible damage done to those children, are we not to think that God did not hear those screams and that he will not call those parents to account? Of course, if there is no God, the answer must be 'no'—those parents will eventually die like the animals of verse 19, since that is how they have acted and that will be the end of it. Although it is interesting to consider that had dogs behaved in this way, we might have just accepted it as 'dog—like behaviour' but since it is *people* we think they *shouldn't* behave like that. Where does *that* idea come from? And so we all have the thought of v. 17, 'I thought in my heart, "*God* will bring to judgement both the righteous and the wicked, for there will be a time for every activity, a time for every deed.' Indeed, he has already moved in this same direction before pulling back when he writes in verse 15, 'Whatever is has already been, and what will be has been before; and God will call the past to *account.*' As we have seen, this is typical of the Teacher, there is no simple, straight linear argument, there is a moving forward and backward, paradox and even contradiction are held in tension for this is what life is like for us 'under the sun'. But this doesn't mean there will not be a point in the future, when what is 'under the sun' is brought 'under heaven' and a final resolution and judgement will take place.

People sometimes point to the existence of evil as an argument *against* the existence of God. But strange though it may seem, this can be turned on its head and the very fact that evil is being perpetrated has been taken by some to point to the existence, or at least the need, for a God who *will* act justly. This is sometimes called 'the argument from damnation.' This is the way Peter Berger puts it: 'It's our experience in which our sense of what is humanly permissible is so fundamentally outraged that the only adequate response to the offence as to the offender seems to be a curse of supernatural dimensions.' He goes on to say that, 'deeds that cry out to heaven also cry out for hell.'[59] In other words, unless there is final and absolute justice, to which our deepest instincts testify should be the case, then all our actions are ultimately rendered meaningless. The kindness of Mother Teresa and the wickedness of Hitler are reduced to the same insignificant level of value. Hitler liked to kill people, Mother Teresa liked to save them—so what's the difference if there is no God to judge between the two? And so the argument goes, only an all powerful, all knowing, all just God can ensure that this *will* happen. 'The evidence that God exists', Winston Churchill once said, 'was the existence of Lenin and Trotsky, for whom hell was needed.'

But for this to be so there has to be *eternity*—life 'under heaven' as well as 'under the sun' which the writer does seem to consider, but is not all that certain about. On the one hand he considers that much of the pain and anguish in life is a means used by God to remind us of our mortality and our kinship with the rest of the animal kingdom, v. 18,

> I also thought, 'As for men, God tests them so that they may see that they are like the animals. Man's fate is like that of the animals; the same fate awaits them both: As one dies, so dies the other. All have the same breath; man has no advantage over the animal. Everything is meaningless. All go to the same place; all come from dust, and to dust all return.'

But there is a seed of doubt which opens up, another possibility, 'Who knows if the spirit of man rises upward and if the spirit of the animal goes down into the earth?'

But *we* can know and here is the reason why: it was the philosopher Wittgenstein, who wrote,

The sense of the world must lie outside the world. In the world everything is as it is or happens as it does happen. In it there is no value—and if there were, it would be of no value. If there is value which is of value, it must lie outside all happening and being-so. For all happening and being-so is accidental. What makes it non-accidental cannot lie in the world, for otherwise this world again would be accidental. It must lie outside the world.[60]

Left by ourselves we can no more find out the purpose of life than a man can pull himself up by his own shoe laces. What we need is for the meaning to be revealed to us from the *outside*. This point has been well illustrated by Jonathan Sacks:

Take a game like football. Some hypothetical visitor from a land to which football has not yet penetrated wants to understand this strange ritual which excites so much passion. You explain the rules of the game, what counts as a foul, what constitutes a goal, and so on. 'Fine,' says the visitor, 'I now understand the game. What I don't understand is why you get so excited about it.' Here you might have to launch into some larger reflection about games as ritualised conflict, and the role of play in rehearsing skills needed in actual conflict. You might even suggest that ritualised conflict reduces the need for actual conflict: the football pitch is a substitute for the battlefield. There is an internal logic of the system ... but the meaning of the system lies elsewhere, and it can only be understood through some sense of the wide human context in which it is set.[61]

The claim of the Bible is that the 'meaning of the system' has been made known to us in a person some 2,000 years ago. It was then that someone else was also known as 'the Teacher', a son of David. His name was Jesus of Nazareth. He too experienced all the limitations, disappointments and the feelings of the vanity of life for 33 years. And yet his was a life marked by peace and contentment, brimful with meaning and purpose as he came to do his heavenly Father's will. He enjoyed food, drink, friendship; full of gratitude to his Father. What is more, he said that he had come that *we* might 'have life in all its fullness (John 10:10)—not a self-centred life for ever taking, but an other-person centred life, concerned with giving, a life following him. And while he suffered the fate of all humans under the sun—death—it could not hold him, he burst from the grave with a transformed body. God has given him all authority over everyone and everything and he is the one who is going to judge each one of us personally on what we have done with God's gift of life (Matthew 28:18; Acts 17:31).

But this is to rush on ahead too quickly. We must allow the Teacher's book to first speak to us in its own terms and to raise questions for us. At this juncture the question we face is: what are we going to do with our lives? Are we going to let it have all the significance and impact of a bubble, a thin spherical film of soap which you hardly notice, or are we going to make it count for something and follow the footprints to their source by tuning in to the signals of transcendence?

Questions for further thought and discussion

What are the big questions you and those around you are asking about life and the universe?

Are there realities about God's world that point you to believe in his existence and at the same time make you confused as to why things are that way?

Look at chapter 3:18–22. How should your frustrations at not understanding affect how you view yourself and humanity?

How does your perspective on the frustrations and injustices of life change when you consider them 'under heaven', that is, with an eternal, God filled perspective?

4

The wind of wealth and worship

Ecclesiastes 5:1–20

In his book, *The American Paradox: Spiritual Hunger in an Age of Plenty*,[62] David Myers notes that Americans are, 'better paid, better fed, better housed, better educated, and healthier than ever before.' Yet alongside this since 1960, the divorce rate has doubled, teenage suicide has tripled, violent crime quadrupled, the number in prison quintupled, illegitimate children sextupled and the number of those cohabiting has increased sevenfold. Similar results have been unearthed by Greg Easterbrook in his book, *The Progress Paradox: How life gets better while people feel worse.*[63] Easterbrook also considers developments in Western Europe. He shows that since the second World War the average American and Western European is wealthier and healthier than all but a handful of people who had ever lived before. Yet, this same period saw an even greater growth of clinical depression. Why? Several reasons are given but Easterbrook notes that the main factor is that, 'many people have lost their belief in higher powers or a higher purpose.' In other words, since there is no God or ultimate purpose to life, we have to try and squeeze some sort of meaning out of the here and now. However, we fail.

Long before Myers and Easterbrook there was the Qoheleth, the Teacher who could have saved them a lot of time and money had they read him because he had already done the research and came to the same conclusions! We read what they are in Ecclesiastes chapter 5.

The great myth which the writer is wanting to expose and burst like the bubble it is—*hebel*—is the myth of fulfilment; the idea that we can gain true satisfaction and significance solely from within *this* world. In this section he takes us to two false tracks which many people are going down: making a religion out of money and making meaninglessness out of religion.

Making a religion out of money—vv. 10–20

Whoever loves money never has enough;
whoever loves wealth is never satisfied with their income.
This too is meaningless.
As goods increase,
so do those who consume them.
And what benefit are they to the owners
except to feast their eyes on them?
The sleep of a labourer is sweet,
whether they eat little or much,
but as for the rich, their abundance
permits them no sleep.

I have seen a grievous evil under the sun:
Wealth hoarded to the harm of its owners,
   or wealth lost through some misfortune,
so that when they have children
there is nothing left for them to inherit.
   Everyone comes naked from their mother's womb,
and as everyone comes, so they depart.
They take nothing from their toil
that they can carry in their hands.

To speak of making a religion out of money is the idea that it becomes the very thing which we look to in order to give us security and significance—what we in effect live for. It defines who we are, what our values should be, what is the main purpose in life. In short, it becomes like a religion—exerting a spiritual power over us to such an extent that it effectively becomes an object of worship. This thought is captured by the saying, 'He who dies with the most toys wins'. No, he doesn't, he is just as dead as the man without any toys, both amount to little more than worm food—v. 15, 'Naked a man comes from his mother's womb, and as he comes, so he departs. He takes nothing from his labour that he can carry in his hand.' However, the prevailing belief in our culture is that money matters such that our whole identity is bound up with what we eat, drink and wear.

What we think is important, is, in part, shown by what we build and invest in terms of our time and energy. During the Middle Ages, cathedrals were built, pointing heavenward to a greater reality; the new cathedrals today are the shopping malls, cathedrals to the god of mammon—sprawling out further and further, devouring more and more space. When my wife and I were in Minneapolis we visited the 'Mall of America'—it is huge; four and half miles of store front footage, eight acres of skylight, and 4.2 million square feet of gross building area. It even had a theme park in the middle of it!

Mike Starkey, in his book 'Born to Shop', develops this religious imagery applied to consumerism:

> Speedbank machines are the wayside shrines where we perform our ritual devotions to the god which motivates us. The icons which offered medieval people the ultimate choice in life have given way to the shelves offering the ultimate consumer choices … In an earlier age, life's adversity was met by robust faith, even if it was only human nature. Today we have our own solution. When the going gets tough, the tough go shopping.[64]

In the 17th century, the philosopher René Descartes is credited with entering a Bavarian 'oven' to contemplate the basis for rational science, resulting in his celebrated statement, *Cogito Ergo Sum*—'I think therefore I am'. Now it is *Tesco ergo sum*—'I shop therefore I am', the basis for irrational significance.

The love of money and trying to find security and satisfaction in more and more things is not anything new, nearly 3,000 years ago our writer warns about it. A thousand years later Jesus made it clear that it was not possible to worship God and mammon (Matthew 6:24). Similarly, the apostle Paul wrote that the 'love of money is the root of all kinds of evil'(1Timothy 6:10). But today through mass marketing, powerful advertising, and simply having a greater amount of disposable income, consumerism is all-consuming. Our children and young people are awash with it. Many Christian parents simply give in to it and then wonder why their children can't take the faith of their parents seriously since their attitude to wealth appears to be hardly any different from that of their friend's parents.

But for all the promises made by the advertisers, wealth can never satisfy. Our writer tells us why.

First, it is *addictive*—v. 10, 'Whoever loves money never has money enough; whoever loves wealth is never satisfied with his income. This too is meaningless.' The Romans had a motto, 'Money is like sea water. The more you drink the thirstier you become.' John F. Rockefeller Sr was asked how much money it takes to make a man happy to which he gave the immortal reply, 'Just a little bit more.' This perceptive observation has been made:

> The current preoccupation with happiness—a massive spate of books in recent years—testifies to a genuine questioning of whether we may not have taken a wrong turn in the unbridled pursuit of economic gain. The consumer society, directed at making us happy, achieves the opposite. It encourages us to spend money we do not have, to buy things we do not need, for the sake of a happiness that will not last. By constantly directing our attention to what we do not have, instead of making us thankful for what we do have, it becomes a highly efficient system for the production and distribution of unhappiness.[65]

There never seems to come a point when we can say 'We have enough'. It's addictive.

Secondly, it is *corrupting*, v. 20, 'He seldom reflects on the days of his life, because God keeps him occupied with gladness of heart.' Despite the fact that whatever wealth we have is a gift of God, very rarely does it cause us to think about him, in fact it tends to have the opposite effect; we spend most of the time thinking about the money and the 'stuff' it buys. The result is that it becomes an idol and, as with all false gods, we become more and more like the gods we worship—in this case shallow.

Andrew Carnegie was the great American multi-millionaire industrialist of the late 19th century. He wrote a famous note to himself in 1868 when he was thirty three years old and stuffed it in a drawer. It said, 'Man must have an idol—the amassing of wealth is one of the worst species of idolatry— no idol is more debasing than the idol of money'. If only he had taken his own note to heart! In 1905 President Theodore Roosevelt reluctantly wrote of Carnegie, 'I have tried hard to like Carnegie, but it is pretty difficult. There is no type of man for whom I feel a more contemptuous abhorrence than for one who makes a God of mere money-making.' We may not have the mountains of money that Carnegie had, but if we are honest, most of us don't do too badly. How much attention are we giving for ourselves and others we may be responsible for, to what we eat, drink and wear—and, we may add, our hobbies or the state of our homes? Remember, these are good things—v. 18,

> This is what I have observed to be good: that it is appropriate for a person to eat, to drink and to find satisfaction in their toilsome labour under the sun during the few days of life God has given them—for this is their lot.

However, they are never to become *the* thing.

G. K. Chesterton put the problem facing us like this: 'A person who is dependent upon the luxuries of this life is a corrupt person, spiritually corrupt, politically corrupt, financially corrupt. Christ said that to be rich is to be in a peculiar danger of moral wreck.' The Christian psychologist Karl Menninger once asked a wealthy patient, 'What on earth are you going to do with all that money?' The patient replied, 'Just worry about it I suppose!' Dr Menninger pressed him further, 'Well, do you get much pleasure out of worrying about it?' 'No' responded the patient, 'but I get such *terror* when I think of giving it to somebody else.' There is the fear of letting go of money because it feels we are letting go of something of ourselves and so our sense of security which is bound up with it. Given the link in our minds between ourselves and our money then it is natural to suppose that the more money we have the more important and secure we feel ourselves to be and the less we will feel our need of God, that is when we tip over into the abyss and are lost. It is corrupting.

Thirdly, it is *self-defeating*, v. 15, 'Naked a man comes from his mother's womb, and as he comes, so he departs. He takes nothing from his labour that he can carry in his hand. This too is a grievous evil: As a man comes, so he departs, and what does he gain, since he toils for the wind? All his days he eats in darkness, with great frustration, affliction and anger.' Death is the great leveller. As we often say, 'You can't take it with you', although the Egyptians strangely thought they could, hence the Pyramids. But of course the only people who really benefitted were grave robbers and the British Museum!

So what are we to do? Verses 18–19 provide the necessary

insight: 'Then I realized that it is good and proper for a man to eat and drink, and to find satisfaction in his toilsome labour under the sun during the few days of life God has given him—for this is his lot. Moreover, when God gives any man wealth and possessions, and enables him to enjoy them, to accept his lot and be happy in his work—this is a gift of God.' We are meant to be thankful for what we have and so contented, with the result that we express our gratitude to the great Giver.

> Ecclesiastes, a man of untold wealth and sophistication ... eventually finds meaning in simple things, love and work, eating and drinking, doing good to others and knowing that there is a time for all things: to be born and to die, to weep and to laugh, to acknowledge the eternity of God and to accept the limits of human life.[66]

Our wealth is not meant to make us forgetful of God, (although in our self-centredness that is often what happens); rather, it is meant to make us mindful of God. Paul's question to the Corinthian Christians is one we should be asking of ourselves on a daily basis: 'What do you have that you did not receive?' (1 Corinthians 4:7). 'Oh,' we say, 'but *I* have worked for this. *I* have put the food on the table. *I* have laboured so hard and so *I* deserve some perks.' Maybe, but who gave you the health so you can work? Who in his Providence enables you to live in a country where such wealth can be generated, if not God? Everything we have can be traced back to his gracious hand. So as God is the gracious giver to us of things we are rightly to enjoy (v. 18), we are to imitate him in this regard and give freely of our wealth to others. Satisfaction is not found in hoarding, getting more and more, it is found in giving, not least to God's work in the service of God's people, which brings us back to the beginning of the chapter and vv. 1–7.

Making meaninglessness out of religion vv. 1–7

But even here we have to be careful lest we make meaninglessness out of religion:

> Guard your steps when you go to the house of God. Go near to listen rather than to offer the sacrifice of fools, who do not know that they do wrong. Do not be quick with your mouth, do not be hasty in your heart to utter anything before God. God is in heaven and you are on earth, so let your words be few. As a dream comes when there are many cares, so the speech of a fool when there are many words. (Ecclesiastes 5:1–3)

He is talking about what happens when a worshipper goes to the temple. In the case of the fool (that is the non-thinking person, the superficial worshipper), the problem is that he takes that which is good—worship of God—and makes it into bubbles, emptiness. This kind of worshipper sees himself at the centre of it all, he is focusing on *his* offering, *his* words and, as far as he is concerned, *he* can dictate terms to God:

> When you make a vow to God, do not delay in fulfilling it. He has no pleasure in fools; fulfil your vow. It is better not to vow than to make a vow and not fulfil it. Do not let your mouth lead you into sin. And do not protest to the temple messenger, 'My vow was a mistake.' Why should God be angry at what you

say and destroy the work of your hands? Much dreaming and
many words are meaningless.   (5:4–7)

The man being depicted has made a promise to do
something, perhaps give some money to the Temple, but then
decides to renege on that vow and feels he has every right to
do so. In other words, worship is about satisfying himself, a
means of allowing him to feel good in offering his sacrifice
and in making vows he doesn't intend to keep. Even when
he is in the temple, he spends a lot of his time not listening
to the sermon but day-dreaming—v. 7, 'Much dreaming and
many words are meaningless.' He expects religion to satisfy
him and doesn't want any religion which might be a personal
inconvenience.

The danger today is for the church to portray Christianity
as if it is all about us rather than God and so create wrong
expectations with the result that our religion becomes a
bubble which is gossamer-light and wafer-thin.

> The problem is in our expectations. It begins in our
> evangelism pitch. Marketing strategies dictate that you have
> to sell the benefits of your product. So we sell Christianity, no
> longer as giving up everything to follow Christ, but finding
> a wonderful, marvellous, happy new life in Christ that is
> characterized by blessing (=health, prosperity and success),
> fellowship (=acceptance and fruitful relationships), peace (=no
> troubles)—the very thing the world promises in advertisements
> … The fulfilment hype shows up in many guises, from the
> obvious excess of the health and wealth gospel to many subtle
> forms. It is always recognizable as it promotes an expectation of
> success, whether of a material sort or in spiritual undertakings.

Christians disappointed by the lacklustre returns on their conversion at times abandon the church and their faith or alternatively wonder what they are doing wrong—where the formula for success broke down. Many blame God for failing to deliver on his promises (though they have forgotten that the promises were made by Christians not by Christ).[67]

In other words, we are not to look to God for self-fulfilment. This kind of religion which, while drawing in the punters, will end up in the same position as everything else under the sun—meaningless, empty, although, like other things, it will satisfy for a while. It is 'Big Mac Religion'.

The largest church in the USA is in Houston, Texas, with a membership of forty thousand. The Pastor, Joel Osteen, regularly teaches what he has written in his best selling book, *Your Best Life Now*. (Even the title gives the game away)

There are seven steps, he says, to 'living at your full potential': 1. Enlarge your vision; 2. develop a healthy self-image; 3. discover the power of your thoughts and words; 4. let go of the past; 5. find strength through adversity; 6. live to give; 7. choose to be happy. What would the writer of Ecclesiastes say of that? 'It is a chasing after the wind'. It is wrapping up the American dream in Christian dress and selling it as the real deal. Of course thousands are going to go and hear that for that is what they *want* to hear. Some churches in the UK do the same, maybe on a smaller scale, but it is the same error—placing man at the centre and pushing God to the margins.

This is a turning inside out and upside down of what really should be the case. When Christians come to the 'house of God' they are meant to 'guard their steps', not traipse in as if it were a concert. The purpose of the gathering is not to tell God what to do, but to listen to him telling us what we should do.

Our world is a world full of chatter, it is the mobile phone, text world, where more and more is being said and less and less of it worth saying.

> Ingmar Bergman once remarked that when God dies in a culture the Church chatters. You can see this in the day of the image, words mean little and they commit people to hardly anything. But traditionally Christians' commitment to God's Word imbibed them with a due sense of seriousness, so that our 'yes's' mean 'yes' and our 'no's' mean 'no'. 'The Lord is in heaven and our words should be few' and we shall be judged or justified according to our words. There should be clarity, cogency and comprehensiveness in a day which is careless in its talk.[68]

The perspective of Ecclesiastes is that God is the centre of *everything*; he gives weight to a weightless world for he is *God*. We do not trivialise him by our words or the way we worship—we stand in awe—v. 7. He is the ultimate reality who does not pass away; neither do his words pass away. It is only being rightly related to him that we can ensure that *we* will not pass away and that our lives will count for something by serving him. It is the eternal word of God which brings eternity into our lives and gives them substance, meaning; it is by Christians meeting regularly that they are reminded that this world is not all there is, it is fleeting, a mere vapour, and there is a world to come—a heaven to gain and a hell to avoid.

The writer Os Guinness makes this telling observation:

When I was young in the faith, regular worship was considered essential. It was both the practice of the ministers and the expectation of the people that the sermon would bring a direct, helpful and practical word from God for his people. In many parts of the West this is no longer the expectation or the practice. Church-going is viewed by many as merely optional; an increasing number of people have no regular experience of sitting under an authoritative word from God; and in many parts of the Western world preaching has fallen on hard times. I have been in mega-churches where there was no cross in the sanctuary and no Bible in the pulpit, and where the sermons refer more to the findings of Barna and Gallup than to those of the Bible or God.

He then goes on to write:

The two greatest preachers I have heard are the great Welshman Martyn Lloyd-Jones, of Westminster Chapel, London, and the great Englishman John Stott of All Souls Langham Place, London. Neither of them prefaced their sermons with, 'This is the Word of the Lord.' But neither needed to. Having prepared before God, come straight from the presence of God, and delivering what they said as from God in the presence of God, their authority was unmistakable and its effect profound. No prophets could have stirred and challenged their audiences more deeply. At the same time, there were many more moments in public worship when it was as if the ceiling was punctured and there was an interruption of the transcendent.

He then offers this challenging question:

Did those who lead the worship pray and expect such a breaking-in of the supernatural in ways we no longer do, even with our improved stage management, our choreography, our dance, our drama and our PowerPoint expositions?[69]

Sadly, it is only too possible to make religion, even 'biblical' religion, meaningless—all froth and bubble with no substance. If God has put eternity on our hearts, then we can be satisfied with nothing less than eternity being brought to us, and, to put it bluntly, that happens when we shut up, God speaks, and we listen and stand in awe.

Questions for further thought and discussion

What emotions come to the surface when you think about money? What does this tell you about its status in your life?

What clarity about wealth and God does chapter 5 give that exposes the worthlessness of money as a god?

Are there things your church family is tempted to do that are essentially foolish and trivial for the sake of being relevant?

How does your approach to God and the approach of your church need to change to avoid empty devotion and cultivate careful, meaning-filled worship?

5

Governments of vapour

Ecclesiastes 8:1–17

Back in 1976 many evangelicals had great hope for the reversal of America's moral decline and firm convictions about just where that hope lay. A relatively unknown candidate had emerged from Georgia to take the country by storm. His name was Jimmy Carter, and he was a Baptist who talked openly about his faith. He even taught Sunday school.

Disillusionment soon set in, however. Even a President who taught Sunday school didn't make a difference. So in 1978 leaders of what is now known as the Religious Right met in Washington to set their own conservative political agenda for the 1980s. Their candidate Ronald Reagan, would be different, they promised. His public charisma and apparent sympathy for their convictions would channel evangelical energies and change the nation.

But as the sun set on the Reagan presidency eight years later, it also set on the hopes of many of these once-euphoric Christians who had overestimated their influence and

underestimated the difficulty of keeping their balance on the
slippery slope of politics. Despite unprecedented access to
the Oval office, they had been unable to implement their
evangelical agenda.[70]

So writes the late Charles Colson. He certainly knew what
he was talking about for he himself had been a President's
right-hand man, Richard Nixon's 'hatchet man' in fact.[71] It
was in the aftermath of the notorious 'Watergate' scandal
that he came to a personal Christian faith (followed by a spell
in prison). Why, then, did Christians become disillusioned?
Colson provides his own thoughts as to the answer; it was
due to a 'disregard for two key truths, first, the solutions to
all human ills do not lie in political structures; and second,
it is impossible to effect genuine political reform solely by
legislation.'[72]

The writer of Ecclesiastes would agree with that assessment.
As we have seen, the Teacher has been exploring what are
the proper and improper expectations we can have as human
beings living 'under the sun', that is living in this good, but
fractured, fallen world. He has been considering whether
we can ever achieve the 'bottom line' in life by gaining real,
substantial satisfaction and value. The Qoheleth has been
searching for someone or something to deliver those goods.
So far he has explored education, work, pleasure, money,
even religion and at every turn when considered in and of
themselves they fail miserably. This is especially so when we
ignore the eternal dimension—'life under heaven'. This is the
perspective that there *is* more to life than what we can wear,
eat, and drink. We all know deep down this to be so, because
God, he tells us, has put 'eternity' into our hearts (3:11). Yet

the frustration is that left to ourselves we can't fathom what this 'something more' is. We need help from the outside. In short, we need special revelation.

However, there is one more arena to which people look in order to solve most, if not all, of their problems, and that is the political forum, the sphere of government. People turn to the so-called 'movers and shakers' of the world to provide the goods. The Teacher himself was one such power-broker for we are told at the beginning of the book that he was a King of Israel. It would have been the easiest thing in the world for him to believe his own publicity about how all-important and all-powerful he was so that he at least would be able to make a difference to people's lives. But, as we have seen, one endearing quality of this man is that he wants the Truth—with a capital 'T' at all costs. Accordingly, he sees it as his responsibility to share the findings of his research so that those who follow don't go down blind alleys and end up being disillusioned because of wrong expectations, including wrong expectations from those who, like himself, govern.

There is little doubt that particularly in the 20th century, right up to the present day, many people have placed great store in politics and the role of government to change the world for the better. This is not entirely misplaced of course. Those in such positions of power do have a responsibility to use it properly for people's good. Without doubt, tremendous changes for the better by any social indicator have been brought about by successive governments in Britain since the Second World War in terms of education, social welfare, health and a whole host of things. But where things start to go wrong is when politics is seen as the tool of an ideology which effectively pushes God out of the picture and establishes man firmly at the centre. We see something of this in the inaugural address of President John F. Kennedy back in 1961 in which he said, 'Since most of the world's troubles have been caused by man most of the problems can be solved by man.' That kind of breezy optimism was sorely put to the test just one year later when the world teetered on the edge of a nuclear conflagration with the Cuban Missile Crisis. Not that much has changed. The predominant outlook is that with the right knowledge, the right resources, and the right will, crime on our streets will be reduced, terrorists will be hunted down, poverty will be abolished and our environment will be made safe.

According to the Teacher, what should our stance be towards government and what might we properly expect as a result?

The proper attitude towards government
vv. 1–6:

Who is like the wise man? Who knows the explanation of things? Wisdom brightens a man's face and changes its hard appearance. Obey the king's command, I say, because you took an oath before God. Do not be in a hurry to leave the king's presence. Do not stand up for a bad cause, for he will do whatever he pleases. Since a king's word is supreme, who can say to him, 'What are you doing?' Whoever obeys his command will come to no harm, and the wise heart will know the proper time and procedure. For there is a proper time and procedure for every matter, though a man's misery weighs heavily upon him.

Here is the wise man's approach which leads to a gracious demeanour, a 'bright face', rather than a sour one. Basically he is saying: serve where you can, obey where you must, and stand apart from injustice.[73] At the one extreme, 'Do not be in a hurry to leave the king's presence' (retreating from the heat) and at the other, 'Do not stand up for a bad cause' (giving in to the standards around you). The Teacher is saying: 'Don't unnecessarily endanger yourself, but don't stand up for a bad cause either; keep a low profile and wait—there will be a proper time and a proper way to do things.'

Sometimes people can be a little too hard on Christians in government because they don't seem to be waving the Christian flag enough or they appear to allow things through by way of legislation which we think do not sit comfortably with the Christian faith. In some instances that might well be true. But we might pause and think of Daniel in the Old Testament. He was in a position of great influence with several pagan kings. There were times, (maybe most of the time) when he simply got on with promoting the welfare of the Empire. You could well imagine some of his fellow Jews complaining that he wasn't doing enough to secure their freedom or improve their lot. But Daniel knew his limitations as to what he *could* achieve. On the other hand, there were times he drew the line in the sand and was willing to pay the ultimate price for it—death (see Daniel chapters 1 and 6). That was a matter of conscience between him and God. As has often been remarked, 'politics is the art of the possible' and some things might be judged not possible, well, not just yet anyway—as we read in verse 5, 'the wise heart will know the *proper time.*' This means that we have to be patient and do what can be done which might not be as much as we had hoped.

What is more, the proper procedure might not be in place. As with the abolition of slavery in the British Empire, it took over 50 years to change attitudes and introduce the necessary legislation. Proper procedure has to be considered.

In Ecclesiastes, of course, we have an absolute monarch and so the extent to which such a king could be influenced was severely limited. We, however, have a democratic system and so the extent to which we can influence government is much greater. But maybe our expectations might be more realistic if, from a biblical viewpoint, we understood the *purpose* of government. At its most basic, the role of government is to restrain evil and promote good. This is what the apostle Paul says in Romans 13:1–6:

> Let everyone be subject to the governing authorities, for there is no authority except that which God has established. The authorities that exist have been established by God. Consequently, whoever rebels against the authority is rebelling against what God has instituted, and those who do so will bring judgement on themselves. For rulers hold no terror for those who do right, but for those who do wrong. Do you want to be free from fear of the one in authority? Then do what is right and you will be commended. For the one in authority is God's servant for your good. But if you do wrong, be afraid, for rulers do not bear the sword for no reason. They are God's servants, agents of wrath to bring punishment on the wrongdoer. Therefore, it is necessary to submit to the authorities, not only because of possible punishment but also as a matter of conscience.

This is also why you pay taxes, for the authorities are God's servants, who give their full time to governing. Give to everyone what you owe them: If you owe taxes, pay taxes; if revenue, then revenue; if respect, then respect; if honour, then honour.

This means that a justice system is needed in order for wrongdoing to be punished. We are not to take the law into our own hands or support injustice, a 'bad cause.' In such a society we surrender some of our basic rights on the understanding that they will be taken up by government on our behalf. For example, we surrender the right to protect our person and property by the use of force on the understanding that the state does it for us instead. Also we expect that if a crime has been committed against us, then that person is punished for it. It is not just a matter of deterrence, nor simply correction, but of justice—deserts. In addition, those who do good in the community should be commended. To some extent it might be said that the honours system in Britain is an attempt to do just that.

Those are the two fundamentals a government should be doing: restraining evil and promoting good.

However, over-reaching expectations are sometimes made of a government which go way beyond what God has in mind. Here is an example which comes from an American junior school textbook, but which could easily have been found in an English one. It claims that over time, 'people were no longer content to live as their forefathers had lived. They wanted richer and fuller lives. They wanted the government to help make their lives rich and full.' Is this not what we hear from our politicians for much of the time: vote for this party and you will have a better deal under us, usually couched in terms of improved public services and personal affluence? But this goes way beyond the concept of limited government whose God-given task it is to ensure the smooth running of society. The name for this is idolatry—making claims which are reserved for God alone.

Jonathan Sacks offers his assessment of what he calls the 'Abrahamic vision' of politics which, not surprisingly, is very much in line with that of the Teacher in Ecclesiastes:

> Politics, in the Abrahamic vision, is not the highest good. It is not where we meet God, nor where we construct our deepest relationships, not where we exercise our highest virtues, not where we achieve individual or national glory. It is a means to an end, no more, no less. It is there to secure peace, security, safety and law-abidingness so that we can get on with our lives, serving God in work and worship, in family and community, arenas we do not entrust to politicians and the state because they require absolute liberty. It is the secondary nature of politics in the Judeo-Christian vision that is the surest guarantor against an intrusive state. Where politics is primary, politicians rule supreme; and where politicians rule, freedom is in danger.[74]

This leads us to seriously consider the limitations of any human government.

The limits of government

vv. 7–8: Since no man knows the future, who can tell him what is to come? No man has power over the wind to contain it (better translation—'over his spirit to retain it'); so no one has power over the day of his death. As no one is discharged in time of war, so wickedness will not release those who practice it.

Sometimes kings and politicians do act as if they have absolute power, but that is an illusion for as Jesus reminded Pilate, whatever power he had was by virtue of God's gift (John 19:11). As an illustration of such limitations the writer focuses on the obvious limitation—death. The ruler has no control over the timing of his own death for example. All his plans and aspirations can come to nothing—if *God* decides his time is up.

This point is amply illustrated by Josef Vissarionovich who was personally responsible for the deaths of over 40 million of his fellow Russian countryman. Of course, he is better known by the name of Stalin, which means 'steel', a name given by his contemporaries who fell under his steel-like will. Stalin once trained for ministry in the church and then made a positive and determined decision to break with his belief in God. Instead he embraced Marxism and became Lenin's notorious successor. Always keen to drive a point home, Stalin once decided to use a visual aid to impress upon his comrades a valuable lesson in social engineering. Forcibly clutching a live chicken in one hand, he systematically started to pluck it with the other. As the chicken struggled in vain to escape, he continued the painful denuding process until the chicken was completely stripped. 'Now watch', Stalin said as he placed the chicken on the floor and walked away with some bread crumbs in his hand. Sure enough, the fear-crazed chicken hobbled towards him and clung to his trousers. Then Stalin threw a handful of grain at the bird and the bird dutifully followed him around the room. He then turned to his henchmen and said, 'This is the way to rule people. If you inflict inordinate pain on them they will follow you for food for the rest of their lives.'[75]

According to his daughter Svetlana, as Stalin lay dying, plagued with terrifying hallucinations, he suddenly sat up halfway in bed, clenched his fist towards heaven, fell back on his pillow and died. So perhaps Stalin was not so much an atheist, but an 'anti-theist'—openly defying the God he really did *know* to exist. It was the God he defied who determined the limits of his life.

It doesn't always follow that the ruler or government has complete power over other people's death either. There is the story of Cornelius Martens which captures this point in a surprising way.[76] Cornelius Martens was in a German Christian community located in Russia during the 1920s. He was quite an evangelist in his day and many people were converted under his ministry. Eventually the communist powers caught wind of this and arrested him. He was thrown into a cell with other dissidents, many being non-Christians, and so he witnessed to them and some were brought to the Christian faith. One day they were all taken out and forced to dig a shallow grave. That night, at around midnight, the prison commandant appeared with a couple of guards and made everyone lie down on their faces. Then he pointed to a prisoner and said, 'Kill him.' So the man was picked up and pushed against the wall and shot. This happened several times and they all thought they were going to be massacred. But eventually it was stopped. A week later, Martens was called into the office of the boss of the local communist party. The official told his two henchmen to take off Martens' clothes.

He said, 'Don't trouble yourself; I will do it for you as I am not afraid to die because I will be going home to the Lord. But if he has decided my hour hasn't come you can't do me any harm here.' That was like waving a red rag to a bull because the official thought that is exactly what he *could* do. He then pulled out his pistol and said, 'I will show you what I can do' and he tried to fire his pistol and nothing happened, his fingers just froze around the trigger and he couldn't pull it. Call it paralysis if you like, but he just couldn't manage to do it no matter how much he tried. His face became redder and redder; he looked like he was going to burst a blood vessel. He tried three times but he just couldn't shoot the gun. God doesn't always do that of course. Usually when guns are fired Christians get killed, but it seemed that God wanted to make a special point in this case.

The fact remains, governments are limited and cannot deliver beyond what God has designed then to deliver. To expect anything more is a chasing after vapour—*hebel.*

The failure of government

Verses 9–15. All this I saw, as I applied my mind to everything done under the sun. There is a time when a man lords it over others to his own hurt. Then too, I saw the wicked buried—those who used to come and go from the holy place and receive praise in the city where they did this. This too is meaningless.

When the sentence for a crime is not quickly carried out, people's hearts are filled with schemes to do wrong. Although a wicked person who commits a hundred crimes may live a long time, I know that it will go better with those who fear God, who are reverent before him. Yet because the wicked do not fear God, it will not go well with them, and their days will not lengthen like a shadow.

There is something else meaningless that occurs on earth: the righteous who get what the wicked deserve, and the wicked who get what the righteous deserve. This too, I say, is meaningless. So I commend the enjoyment of life, because there is nothing better for a person under the sun than to eat and drink and be glad. Then joy will accompany them in their toil all the days of the life God has given them under the sun.

As we have seen, according to the Bible, the basic role of government is to promote the good and restrain evil; nonetheless, together with the Teacher, we are aware that this doesn't always happen. Sometimes the wicked get a funeral with full honours as much as a good man v. 10; proper sentences are not carried out and the wicked seem to get away with too much v. 11; and roles are sometimes reversed so that the good folk get rough justice and the wicked get not justice at all—v. 14. All of this can become quite dispiriting to the citizen and in some cases lead either to open cynicism or outright rebellion. But the Teacher won't have either of these as an option for the believer in God, v. 12, 'I know that it will go better with God-fearing men, who are reverent before God. Yet because the wicked do not fear God, it will not go well with them, and their days will not lengthen like a shadow.' In other words, God will have the last word for final judgement *will* happen.

In the meantime, however, it will often puzzle and vex us as to why God allows this kind of thing to happen. Why should good kings die relatively young, while tyrants can go on for years? That is when governments too seems like smoke, a mere vapour, which is the Teacher's conclusion in v. 16, 'When I applied my mind to know wisdom and to observe man's labour on earth—his eyes not seeing sleep day or night—then I saw all that God has done. No one can comprehend what goes on under the sun. Despite all his efforts to search it out, man cannot discover its meaning. Even if a wise man claims he knows, he cannot really comprehend it.'

It is important to note that our writer does have a strong notion of God's rule v. 17, 'then I saw what *God* has done.' This is a major biblical theme, that the rise and fall of kings and governments all come under the divine decree and *God's* government is the only one which will last for ever and cannot fail.[77] The New Testament knows that divine government by the more familiar term, 'the Kingdom of God'.[78] While it is our duty, as the Teacher has told us in v. 2, to obey the king's command and do all that we can to promote the general welfare of our fellow human beings by all legitimate means, our primary allegiance is to God's government and the two are not to be confused. The Teacher has made it abundantly clear that human government is limited and can achieve only so much. However, God's kingdom doesn't suffer from such limitations and can achieve far more.

These words by former Prime Minister, Margaret Thatcher, delivered to the General Assembly of the Church of Scotland, are certainly pertinent in this context:

> The truths of the Judaic-Christian tradition are infinitely precious, not only, as I believe because they are true, but also because they provide the moral impulse which alone can lead

to that peace ... for which we all long ... There is little hope for democracy if the hearts of men and women in democratic societies cannot be touched by a call to something greater than themselves. Political structures, state institutions, collective ideals are not enough. We parliamentarians can legislate for the rule of law. You the church can teach the life of faith.

Perhaps the most significant phrase is, 'Something greater than themselves' is needed for real change to take place. The Prime Minister speaks of this as a 'moral impulse' and goes on to say:

When all is said and done, a politician's role is a humble one. I always think that the whole debate about the church and the state has never yielded anything comparable in insight to that beautiful hymn 'I vow to thee my country.' It begins with a triumphant assertion of what might be described as secular patriotism, a noble thing indeed in our country like ours: 'I vow to thee my country all earthly things above; entire, whole perfect the service of my love.' It goes on to speak of 'another country I heard of long ago' whose King cannot be seen and whose armies cannot be counted, but 'soul by soul and silently her shining bounds increase.'[79]

The political theorist, Russell Kirk, made the same point albeit differently, 'Politics' he said, 'is the art of the merely possible. The long-run decisions of the electorate are formed not by party platforms and campaign speeches, but by visions, by prejudices if you will. Only the changing of visions can produce large enduring political alterations, for better or worse.'[80] In other words, people need higher aspirations, values, a vision to bring about real, lasting change. This can only take place if *hearts* are changed and no government can do that—but the Christian Gospel can and does.

The relationship between Christians, the Gospel, government and society has been well summarised by Dr Martyn Lloyd-Jones. Speaking to Christians he says:

> If we give the impression that we have no concern about political and social matters we shall alienate people; and I suggest that we have done so, and so the masses are outside the church. On the other hand, if we think we are going to fill our churches and solve our problems by preaching politics and taking an interest in social matters we are harbouring a very great delusion.[81]

Earlier he writes:

> Men must be born again. How can they live the Christian life if they have not become Christians? ... Nevertheless, government and law and order are essential because man is in sin; and the Christian should be the best citizen in the country. The Christian must act as a citizen and play his part in politics and other matters to get the best conditions possible ... and be content with that which is less than Christian.[82]

Those who have changed Britain for the better have been men and women inspired by the values of another government which provided their 'moral impulse'—a greater kingdom—the kingdom of heaven. Whether it is Lord Shaftesbury or William Wilberforce, John Wesley or Elizabeth Fry,[83] they have recognised the value of government and its limitations, but have all been animated by a commitment to a Personal God who has established his kingdom through his Son, the Lord Jesus Christ.

Whatever sins and weaknesses beset the Church, Christians have much to which they can point and say, 'Look at the effects of the kingdom.' Without doubt one of the greatest periods of social improvement was during the latter part of the 18th century and throughout the 19th century. Whereas France endured a bloody revolution in the name of Enlightenment, Britain enjoyed a spiritual revolution under the Evangelicals. But it didn't remain in the heart alone; it translated itself into action to benefit other people. This is what Professor Élie Halévy writes of the abolition of slavery, 'But to understand the delight with which the emancipation of the Negroes was greeted, the rejoicing which took place on a large scale throughout the entire country … we must remember that the abolitionist campaign had been first and foremost a Christian movement.'[84] Or think of improvements in popular education, as mentioned in one of the early editions of the Encyclopaedia Britannica, that this was, 'A striking tribute to the sterling qualities of self help and religious earnestness which were so characteristic of the Early Victorian period.' Improvements in workers' rights and conditions can also be traced back to the influence of the Christian faith. Here is the late Jack Lawson, MP in his book, *A Man's Life*: 'The first fighters and speakers for unions and improved conditions were Methodist preachers. That is beyond argument. And the Gospel expressed in social terms has been more of a driving power in northern mining circles than all the economic teaching put together.'[85]

This is a kingdom which will not disappoint since it is

a kingdom which will outlast all other kingdoms, whose citizens discover that obedience to the commands of this King are good and right and who know that in the end righteousness will reign and wickedness will be dealt with. This is a kingdom for which it is worth giving up everything.[86]

Questions for further thought and discussion

What are your expectations for what the government will achieve? How do they need to be reassessed in the light of Ecclesiastes 8 and Romans 13:1–6?

How should the limits of government shape how and when Christians engage in political campaigns?

What is your natural response to the failure of government—cynicism or rebellion? How should the reality of 'God's government' redeem and reshape your attitude to earthly government?

Consider a political issue that is important to you (e.g. abortion legislation). How could you seek change through political progress? How could you seek change through gospel progress?

6

Grave concerns

Ecclesiastes 9

A pastor is cutting his front lawn. He looks up from his task just in time to see a heavy dump truck back out of his neighbour's driveway—right over the neighbour's eighteen-month old son, who had been squatting behind the huge tires. The pastor accompanies the hysterical mother and ashen father to the hospital in the ambulance. There is no hope for the little boy; he has been crushed beyond recognition—Where is God?[87]

We have to admit that such suffering does not make sense. We might possibly see a plausible connection between certain forms of behaviour and the suffering they occasion, for example, sexual promiscuity and STDs, but what possible connection could there be in terms of *desert* to account for the appalling atrocities undergone by the Jews during the Holocaust? As we contemplate the holocaust in all its naked evil, can we honestly believe that all those children tortured by the Nazis were not in a very real sense *innocent* sufferers? This is when the question is raised in earnest: Where is God?

It was nearly 70 years ago that Auschwitz concentration camp was discovered by the Soviet Army in 1945. One of those found was a 15 year old Hungarian Jewish boy Elie Wiesel. He, his mother and sister were separated at the camp, never to see each other again. He wrote:

> Never shall I forget that night, the first night of the camp, which has turned my life into one long night, seven times cursed and seven times sealed. Never shall I forget that smoke, never shall I forget those flames which consumed my faith forever ... Never shall I forget those moments which murdered my God and my soul and turned my dreams to dust. Some talked of God, of his mysterious ways, of the sins of the Jewish people, and of their future deliverance. But I ceased to pray. How I sympathised with Job! I did not deny God's existence, but I doubted his absolute justice.[88]

Behind the cry 'Where is God?' is the deeper cry of Wiesel, 'Where is God's justice?' In the case of the true story of the anguished parents of the little boy accidently run over by his Dad, is the plea 'Why did God allow it to happen?' It seems so unfair, so unloving, so meaningless.

Sometimes believers in the God of the Bible are accused of looking at the world through rose-tinted spectacles. Only that which is good and the beautiful are seen; the bad and the ugly are simply filtered out. How else is a believer's faith to remain intact when it is confronted with misery, evil and rank injustice? That might be a question we would want to put to the Teacher. What is striking to observe is that as the Qoheleth ploughs on relentlessly, chapter after chapter, concluding that everything is mist—*hebel*—his faith in God *does* remain intact and shows no signs of diminishing. He can hardly be accused of wearing rose coloured glasses! In particular, it is when he faces up to the great leveller, 'death' and what appears to be the sheer randomness of life where the good is not always rewarded and the bad seems to thrive, that in spite of the absurdity of it all, the call is still to look to God and to enjoy his benefits. This is the great theme of chapter 9.

The mockery of death

Today there is a tendency to romanticise death. Not only do we use euphemisms such as 'passing away' to avoid the 'D' word, but we wrap up its cold reality with hazy, hopeful notions that all will be well in the 'sweet by and by'. That is not the way of the Teacher:

> So I reflected on all this and concluded that the righteous and the wise and what they do are in God's hands, but no one knows whether love or hate awaits them. All share a common destiny—the righteous and the wicked, the good and the bad, the clean and the unclean, those who offer sacrifices and those who do not.
> As it is with the good,
> so with the sinful;
> as it is with those who take oaths,
> so with those who are afraid to take them.
> This is the evil in everything that happens under the sun: The same destiny overtakes all. The hearts of people, moreover, are full of evil and there is madness in their hearts while they live,

and afterward they join the dead. Anyone who is among the living has hope even a live dog is better off than a dead lion!

For the living know that they will die,
but the dead know nothing;
they have no further reward,
and even their name is forgotten.
Their love, their hate
and their jealousy have long since vanished;
never again will they have a part
in anything that happens under the sun. (9:1–6)

Gordon Reece and his wife were invited to a dinner party at a trendy suburb in Sydney, Australia, in order to discuss Christianity. At once stage, after listening to a number of idealised theories about reincarnation—likening death to birth—the wife spoilt the entire evening by declaring, 'Death is disgusting!' The immediate response, especially from two people who had recently lost loved ones, was, 'No, it's a normal part of life, and while it is difficult it's alright as long as you've both grieved appropriately and come to terms with each other.' Gordon Reece insisted that his wife was correct. Death has a sting and no amount of therapy can remove it. Death is disgusting.[89]

The writer of Ecclesiastes would agree. The 'evil under the sun' is, as he puts it, that the 'same destiny overtakes them all.' The righteous and the wicked both end up occupying graves, maybe even the same grave. There seems to be no correlation between the way they have lived and the way they die. It is proverbial: 'As it is with the good, so with the sinful; as it is with those who take oaths, so with those who are afraid to take them.' (v. 2) Death does not seem to right the wrongs of life or mitigate the 'evil in men's hearts'. Death is not very discriminating, it is impartial. Indeed, it would seem that clinging to life at all costs is the preferable option—'better a live dog than a dead lion.'

The Teacher looks at reality with both eyes wide open and admits that even personal piety is no safeguard, 'All share a common destiny ... the clean and the unclean, those who offer sacrifices and those who do not.' The priest and the pimp, the judge and the junkie—death is no respecter of persons.

It is what has been called 'the terror of randomness'[90] which underscores the evil under the sun which our writer perceives as another instance of *hebel*. This was the experience of Jerry Sittser:

> He remembered an earlier conversation with his wife about an accident reported in their local newspaper. It haunted him now. A station wagon driven by a mother had skidded off the road, killing three of her six children. 'We shivered with fear' he recalled of the conversation with his wife, 'before the disorderliness of tragedy.'[91]

For Sittser, it was not simply that something bad had happened, but that it had happened so randomly, there being no rhyme or reason which could remotely be conceived. Then it happened to Sittser himself as he lost his mother, wife and one of his children in a car accident caused by a drunk driver.[92] Life is unpredictable and so, in the main, people are unprepared. Life is not fair; indeed, listening to the Qoheleth one would be hard pressed to draw any other conclusion than that it is cosmically unfair. Under the sun, life, in the face of death, can be terrifying—it is certainly *hebel*.

Of course, what adds to the apparent absurdity and pain of suffering and death is the context of normality in which they occur, namely, joy and life. The Teacher has made reference to these throughout his essay, and even here encourages a delight in such things—v. 7, 'Go, eat your food with gladness, and drink your wine with a joyful heart, … v. 8 Always be clothed in white, and always anoint your head with oil. v. 9 Enjoy life with your wife, whom you love, all the days of this meaningless life.'

> So a family loses its young mother to breast cancer while, a block away, neighbours are rolling with laughter at a television comedy. A middle-aged man despondently leaves his office for the last time, retired early with blank indifference, while outside on the street people are just strolling by. Or a torturer's victim spits out blood from his battered mouth while in the café next door to the police station two lovers are gazing into each other's eyes over a glass of wine. Life just goes on. The cries of our hearts are unheard, and the loneliness adds to the pain.[93]

It is this tension and incongruity between the life and death, pleasure and pain that renders all such things under the sun—*hebel* as insubstantial as bubbles or a curling wisp of smoke.

If life (and death) under the sun is all that there is, the only perspective because, according to the secular humanist we live in a 'universe without windows', it is difficult to see where the protests come from when facing suffering. Who is the atheist shaking his fist at—the God he doesn't believe in? If there is no God, and so no absolute basis for right and wrong, without having a sufficient warrant for distinguishing the value of pain from the value of joy, then suffering, and the grief it occasions, are mere data of existence like the redness of a sunset or the wetness of water—they are just *there*. We can no more object to the presence of suffering than we can to the presence of the wind. The 'problem of pain' appears to be a problem for the believer because of what he affirms about God, viz., that he is good and almighty. The trilemma was originally put forward by Epicurus, 'Is God willing to prevent evil, but not able? Then he is impotent. Is he able but not willing? Then he is malevolent. Is he both able and willing? Whence evil?'[94] Or, in the more familiar words of John Hick: 'If God is perfectly loving and good he must wish to abolish evil; if God is all powerful he must be able to abolish evil. But evil exists therefore God cannot be both perfectly good and almighty.'[95]

The questions of Epicurus and Hick seem a little removed from the way of the Teacher. He would be able to sympathise more with the down to earth anguished cries of those wrestling with the absurdity and the 'why?' questions. Here is C. S. Lewis as he looked upon in anguish at the struggles of his wife Joy Davidman, dying of cancer:

> Tonight all the hells of young grief have opened again: the mad words, the bitter resentment, the fluttering in the stomach, the nightmare unreality, the wallowed-in-tears. Meanwhile where is God? This is one of the most disquieting symptoms. When you are happy … and turn to him in gratitude and praise, you will be welcomed—so it feels—with open arms. But go to him when your need is desperate, when all other help is in

vain, and what do you find? A door slammed in your face, and a sound of bolting and double-bolting on the inside. After that silence.[96]

Rabbi Harold Kushner raised similar agonising questions after his son, Aaron had been diagnosed with a rapid-ageing disease, becoming like an old man of eighty:

> I believed that I was following God's ways and doing his work. How could this be happening to my family? If God existed, if he was minimally fair, let alone loving and forgiving, how could he do this to me? And even if I could persuade myself that I deserved this punishment for some sin of neglect or pride that I was not aware of, what grounds did Aaron have to suffer?[97]

Perhaps even more candid in his questions is Philip Yancey when he writes, 'If God is truly in charge, somehow connected to all the world's suffering, why is he so capricious, so unfair? Is he the cosmic sadist who delights in watching us squirm?'[98]

What might come as a surprise, given the 'no holds barred' nature of the Qoheleth's observations, is that he does *not* raise questions about God's goodness. The evil of such things are acknowledged (v. 3), but the blame is not laid at God's door.

It is highly likely that Genesis 1–3 has influenced the Teacher's thinking and shaped his beliefs, not least that death is, in some way, to be regarded as God's judgement upon sin (Genesis 2:17; 3:19; cf. Ecclesiastes 3:20; 12:7). He appears content to leave matters there.[99] But there is another aspect of the teaching of Genesis which may also have influenced the Teacher which enabled him (and may well enable us), to come to terms with the apparent randomness of suffering and death—the sovereignty of God. We shall return to this below.

The confusion of chance

In addition to the apparent iniquity and absurdity that the shadow of death casts over human existence, is the iniquity and absurdity of what can be called 'chance events'.

> I have seen something else under the sun:
> The race is not to the swift
> or the battle to the strong,
> nor does food come to the wise
> or wealth to the brilliant
> or favour to the learned;
> but time and chance happen to them all.
>   Moreover, no one knows when their hour will come:
> As fish are caught in a cruel net,
> or birds are taken in a snare,
> so people are trapped by evil times
> that fall unexpectedly upon them. (9:11–12)

It might be helpful at this point to clear away any misunderstanding or misapprehension concerning the notion of 'chance'. Sometimes 'Chance' (with a capital 'C') is put forward as an alternative causal explanation to God. But this is really a false alternative with which we are being presented. Chance is simply a word we use to describe events—like tossing a coin—which either has no discernable order or no discernable cause which *we know*. That doesn't mean such things are not known to God. Furthermore, 'Chance' is not some metaphysical 'Other', a positive force which is to be pitted against God. To suppose such a thing would be to make a logical blunder. Chance is not an alternative to God— 'God *or* Chance'—but rather, what we call chance comes under God's sovereign care and design just as much as other things which we can predict more accurately—like the rising and setting of the sun. He is Lord of all. Such a belief arises straight out of the Book of Genesis amongst other places.[100] In the words of Michael Eaton, 'On the lips of an Israelite 'chance' means what is unexpected, not what is random.'[101]

The Teacher is not saying that nothing can be *predicted,* after all, he has already celebrated the patterns of life in chapter 3, so there is a 'time' for everything. However, he is saying that nothing can be *certain* when it comes to human endeavours. We are to 'expect the unexpected'. Even the life of faith is not a life of guarantees. Christians get ill together with non Christians. The pious get caught up in the fall-out of evil as much as anyone else, after all, Christians died in the Twin Towers too. Verse 12, 'As fish are caught in a cruel net, or birds are taken in a snare, so people are trapped by evil times that fall unexpectedly upon them.'

It might be reasonable to gamble on a thoroughbred winning a race, but even that is not a 'dead cert' (as the bookies will tell you) v. 11. There is so much which is unknown to us and strikes us as unfair. Surely the scholar who has the highest IQ and worked the hardest should glean the most prizes? Not necessarily—v. 11—he may have a 'bad hair day' like the rest of us when it comes to final examinations. 'Critical realism' is the name of the game for the Teacher.

And so contrary to the charge sometimes brought against

the man of faith that he has to adopt a Pollyanna attitude
to life to keep going, the Teacher acknowledges that life is
not always fair, it is unpredictable and at times downright
confusing. This view stands in stark contrast to 'Darwin's
Bulldog', T. H. Huxley:

> The ledger of the Almighty is strictly kept, and every one
> of us has the balance of his operations paid over to him at
> the end of every minute of his existence. Life cannot exist
> without certain conformities to the surrounding universe—that
> conformity involves a certain amount of happiness in excess of
> pain. In short, as we live we are paid for living ... The absolute
> justice of the system of things is clear to me as scientific fact.[102]

Who is Huxley trying to fool? How can anyone looking at
the world say, 'we are paid for living?' That absolute justice is
'as clear as scientific fact'?

It is questionable whether his friend Charles Darwin would
have agreed with this assessment when confronted with
the tragic death of his ten year old daughter Annie in 1851.
During his little girl's illness, Darwin was at her bedside
night and day. He was deeply devoted father. Her death
gave poignant meaning to his developing notions of the
callousness of nature and the struggle of all creatures for
survival. For Darwin, death was a *purely natural* process,
part of the machinery of life that drove evolution towards
'endless forms most beautiful.' The only comfort he had over
the loss of Annie was that during her brief life he had never
spoken a harsh word to her, which is not much consolation at
all. There certainly wasn't any belief that he or his wife were
being 'paid for living'.

What, then, enabled the Teacher to retain his faith in God despite the absurdities and injustices of life? It was his view of God, which, as we have seen, is rooted in the first few chapters of the Bible.

The governance of God

What God is doing in his world may be confusing but it is hardly capricious. God is not an absentee landlord who has wound up the universe and let it go its own sweet (and sometimes bitter) way. The God of the Bible, while being distinct from the world ('God is in heaven and you are on earth' 5:2), is nonetheless intimately involved with the patterns of the seasons reflecting something of his providential rule (1:6f). Even the language used here in v. 1 speaks of concerned, divine rule, 'what they do are in God's *hands*'. Providence implies purpose, and although there will be times when the specific purpose of what God is doing at any given moment may be hidden from us ('the good man dying alongside the bad man'—v. 2), God's overall purpose has been revealed together with what our duty is whatever the circumstances: 'Fear God and keep his commandments, for this is the whole duty of man.' So writes the editor of Ecclesiastes having pondered carefully what the Teacher has been saying throughout.

So, to the question: 'How can I stand it?' in a world riddled with pain and injustice, as well as pleasure and righteousness, two answers present themselves.

The first is down-to-earth and practical—we are to get on with the business of living v. 7ff:

> Go, eat your food with gladness, and drink your wine with
> a joyful heart, for God has already approved what you do.
> Always be clothed in white, and always anoint your head with
> oil. Enjoy life with your wife, whom you love, all the days of
> this meaningless life that God has given you under the sun—all
> your meaningless days. For this is your lot in life and in your
> toilsome labour under the sun. Whatever your hand finds
> to do, do it with all your might, for in the realm of the dead,
> where you are going, there is neither working nor planning nor
> knowledge nor wisdom.   (9:7–10)

When the writer and philosopher Iris Murdoch, (who
was wonderfully portrayed in the movie 'Iris' by Dame Judy
Dench) showed signs of sliding into Alzheimer's disease, her
husband, John Bayley, divided their days into simple and
yet discrete units—posting a letter, going for a walk etc. This
was something which could be handled; it was very much a
matter of taking things 'one day at a time'. Bayley would cite
Jane Austen's kind clergyman friend, the Reverend Sydney
Smith, who would counsel members of his flock who were
gripped by depression, 'take short views of human life—never
further than dinner or tea.' It is at points like these we can
utter the honest prayer: 'Father, I may not understand you—
help me to trust you.'

However, it would be difficult and, some would argue
irresponsible, to trust a God who is not in sovereign control
and who does not have the 'righteous and the wise' in his
hands (v. 1). This ties in with the deeper issue of how human
beings are enabled to conduct their days 'under the sun'.

'He who has a why to live for can bear almost any how',
wrote the nihilistic philosopher Friedrich Nietzsche. It was

this thought which was taken up by Viktor Frankl, who himself experienced the horrors of a Nazi concentration camp, in order to develop his treatment called 'logotherapy'. It was here of all places that he noticed the positive way in which some people approached their tragic and horrifying situation. This observation led him to quote Nietzsche with approval when he said that 'Men and women can endure any amount of suffering so long as they know the "why" to their existence'. In other words, if the suffering can be placed within some wider context of meaning and purpose, much, but by no means all, of the sting of mental anguish is relieved. What often makes suffering so morally objectionable is its occurrence in a form which is wholly negative and irrational, apparently devoid of any significance. It is this which lies at the root of so many tormented human cries—'Why should my ten day old baby die?' 'Why should such a gifted man be reduced to a mere shell through cancer?' It is this seeming lack of *purpose*, what is often referred to by philosophers as 'dysteleological' suffering that provides the twist which calls for such pain to be viewed as evil.

From a purely humanistic perspective such suffering cannot but remain meaningless, unless one invokes an evolutionary explanation along the lines of the 'survival of the fittest' requiring suffering. This, as we have seen, was Charles Darwin's agonizing dilemma which brought him no comfort in the loss of his daughter. But if, as the Bible continually asserts and our writer both implicitly and explicitly believes, there is a sovereign God who has purposes in pain, although not always revealed to us, then even when we don't know 'why' we can at least begin to 'trust the God who knows why'.[103]

Indeed, Charles Darwin's wife, Emma, provides a good example of this humble attitude. She was a Christian who sought some *divine* meaning behind her little daughter's death. She believed that God was all wise and good, and although she could not see why he had permitted this, she still trusted that he knew best and that our understanding of God's purposes is limited. Emma could imagine her little Annie in heaven, but Darwin could not. In a sense Charles Darwin saw things with only 'one eye'—the eye of science: the development of life from the inside, the biological mechanism producing greater numbers and more varied life forms which he allowed *could* be taken as God's activity in and through the world. But Emma Darwin was 'two eyed'; so whilst recognizing fully the work of God from the inside of his creation, she also knew of God coming into his creation from the outside in the person of his Son, Jesus Christ, for she had the additional eye of faith, she had the perspective of 'life under heaven' as well as 'life under the sun.'[104]

Another example of someone who embraced the attitude of the Book of Ecclesiastes was the late Dr Lewis Smedes.[105] For twenty five years he was the much-loved Professor of Theology and Ethics at Fuller Theological Seminary, one of the most eminent colleges in the United States. During his retirement he continued to preach and pastor in his denomination, eventually dying aged 81. His seminary President said 'He embodied a unique blend of intellectual rigor, pastoral warmth and eloquent expression. More than one of his former students has said that while his class lectures were unforgettable, it was worth coming to class just to hear his opening prayer.' This is an experience he had in his old age:

My wife Doris and I were winding up a sabbatical at St. John's University in Collegeville, Minnesota. It was getting near Christmas time, cold, real cold, and a wind chill factor of 40 below zero, and it was the morning for us to pack up and head on home to California. Well, I had not slept well that night and was not feeling quite right in the morning. And Doris, alert to how I looked, put on her boots and went out to ask the folks at the University how to get a doctor, just in case I needed one. Well, when she came back she found me lying on the kitchen floor, belly up, my face a battleship gray, eyes wide open but not looking at anything. I was, to be blunt about it, looking very convincingly dead. Doris did all the things she had learned in first aid class, and then called an ambulance. The paramedics loaded me aboard and she climbed aboard, too; and we skidded along the icy road to the emergency room of the hospital in St. Cloud. There they found that my lungs were peppered with blood clots, a killer situation for sure. They told me later that I had no better than one chance in twenty to pull through. But a few mornings after I arrived, a gentle type of physician—from Lake Woebegone, I think!—leaned over my bed and said to me: 'Mr Smedes, congratulations! You have survived something more deadly than the worst heart attack conceivable.' Well, I had not been planning on dying so I was not all that surprised to be alive, and I closed my eyes and went back to sleep. A few nights later, however, in that melancholy hush that settles over the intensive care ward in a hospital at two o'clock in the morning, it happened. No warning. No preparation. Alone in the dark, my spirit was possessed by gratitude. It came on me like a seizure; a fit of frenzy; of pure, unadulterated joy. I became an instant Pentecostal! I waved my arms and shook my hands in a delirium of gratitude. I must tell you; it was not that I had beaten the 20 to 1 odds against my survival. That wasn't it. It was just the incredible gift of life that I'm given every moment. I felt like a fragile bubble floating in the air, held aloft by nothing but the breath of God. I knew that a little pin prick could break the bubble, and will one day, and I'd be a goner. But God was keeping for now, keeping on breathing the breath of life into me. And life keeps coming. It won't always come, but for this day, for now, for right now, it's enough. Life is such a delicious, miraculous gift. I had been so busy doing things, saying things, that I'd almost forgotten how mysterious and how amazing it is to be alive in this world of such incredible beauty. And now the joy of it came to me full force in a whirlwind of gratitude and all I could say, over and over again, were the words of Psalm 103: 'Bless the Lord. Bless the Lord, O my soul, and everything that is in me bless his Holy Name.'

He died a few years later after falling from a step-ladder while putting up lights on a Christmas tree. He has said, 'I felt like a fragile bubble floating in the air, held aloft by nothing but the breath of God. I knew that a little pin prick could break the bubble, and will one day, and I'd be a goner. But God was keeping for now, keeping on breathing the breath of life into me. And life keeps coming. It won't always come, but for this day, for now, for right now, it's enough.' This is very much the language of Ecclesiastes, but cast in the light of the Gospel. No doubt there were people who thought an eminent servant of God should not end his life in that way, even that the manner of his death in some way put in doubt the faith of his life ('As it is with the good man so it is with the sinner … the same destiny overtakes them all'). But it didn't bring his faith into question and he knew it couldn't no matter whenever and however the end came. He was ready, God was ready, and the fall from the ladder was not the last word in our uncertain world and precarious lives where many things fall from ladders: but no one falls from the hands of the One who holds all the ladders!

'The righteous and the wise are in God's hands'—this gives assurance in the midst of a life which feels like a bubble.

Questions for further thought and discussion

What answers to the 'problem of suffering' does the world around you offer?

As the reality of death has broken into your life and of those around you, what have you concluded about God and human existence? Does it chime with the Teacher's conclusions?

When life feels as fragile as a bubble because of death, how will Ecclesiastes help you face this?

1 Corinthians 15:55—'Where, O death, is your victory? Where, O death, is your sting?'

How does the reality of Jesus Christ and his resurrection shape how we experience death 'under heaven'?

7

Getting through life

Ecclesiastes 10:1–11:8

'Goodbye!' said Gandalf to Thorin. 'And goodbye to you all, goodbye! Straight through the forest is your way now. Don't stray off the track! If you do, it is a thousand to one you will never find it again and never get out of Mirkwood and then I don't suppose I or anyone else will ever see you again.' 'Do we really have to go through?' groaned the hobbit. 'Yes, you do!' said the wizard. 'If you want to get out the other side. You must go through or give up your quest. And I am not going to allow you to go back now, Mr Baggins. I am ashamed of you for thinking of it.'

So writes J. R. R. Tolkien in the Hobbit.[106]
What Tolkien portrays here can be likened to a believer who has to make his journey through this confused and confusing world with all its riches to enjoy and pitfalls to avoid. The question arises: how do you stay on track? What is to prevent us from wandering off and getting lost so that we

will 'never be seen again'? If we have to go through the forest (and the writer of Ecclesiastes would no doubt assent to this picture of life with attendent dangers everywhere, a journey we have no option but to make), is there any guide which might help us see it through to our final destination?

The Teacher is confident that there is, and it is the way of wisdom.[107]

For the Bible, having wisdom is more than having information; it is having the ability to use that knowledge properly. Wisdom is the art of cultivating those skills and virtues which enable us to live in God's world, God's way. That means first of all seeing the world aright, viewing it as God sees it—a good world which operates both on the physical and moral level according to certain laws and principles and we are to fit in with those. It also recognises that it is a scarred and fractured world, broken and dislocated by the effects of sin. What is more, it is a world which is the theatre of a spiritual war which we ignore at our peril. So wisdom is both *descriptive and prescriptive*. The wise person sees things as they are (at least in part) and then seeks to act accordingly. So there are wise ways of doing things which have good effects and foolish ways which have harmful effects. Growing in wisdom involves gaining the ability to discern which is which. It is something more to do with character than with that which is cerebral.

Part of that discernment involves recognising the limits of wisdom. Partly because of our finitude (we can't see the whole picture or know all that we need to know) as well as our corruption (we sometimes don't *want* to know things because they cut across our desires), wisdom can take us only so far. We cannot get everything taped (especially God). This is acknowledged by our teacher of wisdom, the Qoheleth, near the very beginning of his work:

> I, the Teacher, was king over Israel in Jerusalem. I applied my mind to study and to explore by wisdom all that is done under the heavens. What a heavy burden God has laid on mankind! I have seen all the things that are done under the sun; all of them are meaningless, a chasing after the wind.
> What is crooked cannot be straightened;
> what is lacking cannot be counted.
> I said to myself, 'Look, I have increased in wisdom more than anyone who has ruled over Jerusalem before me; I have experienced much of wisdom and knowledge.' Then I applied myself to the understanding of wisdom, and also of madness and folly, but I learned that this, too, is a chasing after the wind.
> For with much wisdom comes much sorrow;
> the more knowledge, the more grief. (1:12–18)

But it is possible to misconstrue the way of wisdom such that it fails to be used properly and ends up being more of a hindrance than a help. This is when principles and general observations are transmuted into cast iron rules, a 'one size fits all' approach, when it patently does not. The most glaringly obvious example of this is the stance of Job's 'friends'. They had bought in to the idea that God simply operates a rewards/retribution principle according to which good people get a good life and bad people get a bad life. They saw a strict cause and effect moral mechanism operating within God's universe similar to the law of gravity, what goes up must come down, good must be rewarded and evil punished. This was the way of 'wisdom' for them, based, they claimed, on received tradition and observation. But Job was cast very much in the same mould as the Teacher; he wasn't going to kowtow to such simplistic (and cruel) notions. He too realised that life was messy and that there was such a thing as *innocent* suffering. The book of Job, like the book of Ecclesiastes, is, in many ways, a corrective to a way of 'wisdom' which ends up as folly and underscores the truth that we don't have the full picture and things don't always fit in a neat and tidy fashion however much we might wish it were otherwise. Life is both messy and mysterious.[108]

This is the way one writer summarises the wisdom approach of the Teacher:

> Qoheleth, mounts a frontal attack on our misguided attempts to master life by pointing out life's limits and mysteries. Wisdom, according to the Book of Proverbs (12:5), involves the 'art of steering' (cf. the translation of the New Jerusalem Bible, 'the art of guidance'). Wisdom helps one pilot oneself through the contradictions of life, much like a boat sailing down a fjord that contains rocks, both seen and submerged.
>
> Observations easily morph into instructions, however. Once voiced, they can become absolutised, if not by the creators, then by the succeeding generations of followers. What begins as an art form—as the recording of observations on life—degenerates into cold calculation and hard work. Life's mystery and grace are in the process robbed of their charm.
>
> The writer of Ecclesiastes seeks to set a limit on wisdom in this regard. Life is not a matter of hard work; its meaning does not open up before us like a problem being solved. Rather, wisdom is more like a flower blossoming forth into beauty. There is some order and regularity, but life's mystery and grace

elude our grasp. Pluck it—remove it from the dirt—and death results.[109]

And so in chapter 10 through to the early part of chapter 11, the Teacher sets out to do his work as an instructor of wisdom, bearing in mind the caveats mentioned above.

'As my old Pappy used to say'

The 1960s was the heyday of Westerns on TV. Programmes like *Wagon Train*, *Bonanza*, and *Rawhide* ensured that little boys like me were glued to the Telly night after night. One of my all-time favourites was a show called *Maverick* starring James Garner, later to be made into a film of the same name with Mel Gibson. *Maverick* was the first TV comedy Western which centred on the card-gambling, fast-talking Maverick brothers, Bret and Bart. Often in the programme the Maverick boys would recount the advice of their father, whom they always called 'Pappy'. There thus developed what came to be known as 'Pappyisms' For example, 'My old pappy would say, "if ever you see trouble coming, turn tail and run."' 'As my old Pappy said, "Never cry over spilt milk, it could have been whisky."' Or, (one of my favourites), 'A coward dies a thousand times. A brave man dies just once. A thousand to one is pretty good odds.' Pithy one-liners from a father to a son in order to provide guidelines to help his offspring get through life with a view to coming out on top. Proverbs operate in a similar fashion; indeed, they are often couched in the form of paternal advice.[110] But these are not just tit bits of worldly wisdom picked up along the way in some haphazard fashion; they are the sayings of a man whose life has been shaped by God. What is being promoted is not so much the 'good life', although it is that, but the 'God life' that is, the God-centred, God-directed, God-driven life, for the end of this book parallels the beginning of the Book of Proverbs. In Proverbs it is, 'The fear of the Lord is the beginning of knowledge' (Proverbs 1:7), In Ecclesiastes it is, 'Fear God and keep his commandments.' (Eccl.12:13).

So what sort of sayings will help us through a world which consists of a good deal of 'mist'—*hebel*?

Stand up in court

First, it is important to appreciate the context from which the Teacher is speaking and into which he is speaking. It is the royal court. This is the place where power tended to reside in the ancient Near East and where wisdom was meant to be displayed (given that the stakes were often high, the well-being or downfall of a kingdom), but where folly would sometimes get the upper hand. Many of the proverbs the Qoheleth is about to unfold find their home there. Our situation is somewhat different; power and influence are more diffused throughout society and so to a greater or lesser extent we all find ourselves in positions of responsibility and influence—in the classroom or the boardroom, the shop floor or the city hall—and wisdom to negotiate our way through is crucial, especially if we want to live a God-centred life.

Watch your step

Chapter 10:1,

> 'As dead flies give perfume a bad smell,
> so a little folly outweighs wisdom and honour.'

The surface reading of the proverb seems straight forward. We even talk of the 'fly in the ointment', a little something which can ruin a good thing. And so it may be here. A good life can be marred by a wrong action. We can all think of examples where the career of a public figure—a politician or a preacher—is suddenly destroyed by a scandal. This is all the more tragic if it takes place towards the end of a life. Whatever honour may have been accrued during the rest of their life is forgotten and overshadowed by that one moment of foolish indiscretion. That is certainly when a life is vaporised into *hebel*.

But the original language is a little obscure at this point[111] and suggests an altogether different interpretation. When you think about it, the decay of a fly in a jar of perfume is hardly going to affect the scent being given off by the ointment. Any effect would be marginal. But the picture could be that of a dead body which is being infested by flies leading to putrefaction and the giving off of a stench which is masked by perfumes, but not sufficiently. What is more, the original line seems to bring together stench and perfume within the context of *words*. That is, words of folly which have the odour of wisdom. Therefore, a ruler may make a pronouncement which sounds so plausible and appealing, having the appearance of wisdom, but which turns out to be folly; words which hide the stench of death.

The perfume of fine words has done much throughout the 20th century to mask philosophies and ideas which have led to nothing but untold misery and destruction.

Let us take just one example of someone who has changed the West's outlook on sex and especially homosexuality, perhaps more than any other by using the perfumed words of academia and 'science', the American zoologist Alfred Kinsey. In 1948 and 1953 he produced two very influential reports which, amongst other things, claimed that 10% of the male population were predominately homosexual. Did Kinsey pursue his studies with scientific detachment with no axe to grind? Not according to his biographer James H. Jones.[112] Kinsey himself was both homosexual and a sadomasochist who encouraged his research team to have sex with each other and his wife, which he filmed in their attic. He also fixed his research results to support his lifestyle. Far from taking representative samples from the male population at large to determine sexual orientation and practice, 26% of his subjects were sex offenders and a further 25% were in prison, the rest were male prostitutes and pimps. Worse still, is the more recent evidence that he employed and trained paedophiles. This work provided much of the basis for the loosening of society's attitudes towards sexual activity from the 1960s to the present time. Do you see what was driving this scientific research? Certainly, not the pursuit of objective truth, but sadly his own desires. And yet his views are still held in public high esteem even today, though his work has been effectively discredited; academically perfumed words masking the stench of moral decay.

Let's take one tragic instance of this; the rise in teenage abortions. Now over 3,500 girls under 16 have their pregnancies terminated in the UK each year. Think, then, of how many are actively involved in under-age sex. Add to this the undermining of parental responsibility for children, for now they are being offered abortions without their parents' consent. The result? Not only a rise in pregnancies but of sexually transmitted diseases. This comes in part from the thinking of that children are mini-adults when they are not. Here is Melanie Phillips commenting on these trends:

> What they (Children) actually need are firm boundaries that tell them certain behaviour is wrong and that it inevitably carries unpleasant consequences. But instead, when it comes to alcohol, drugs and sex, the adult world has ripped up those boundaries and effectively told children to go ahead and indulge—provided they are careful—and then express mortification when they are not. Some influential people actively want to promote a breakdown in conventional norms of behaviour. Many other in official circles believe—wrongly—that government is helpless to resist the great cultural movement towards a behavioural free for all.

Dangerous ideas and the sweet words which convey them are very powerful and the Teacher is urging his readers to be aware of these and so become discerning.

How, then, are those who wish to follow the way of wisdom to conduct themselves when such perfumed, death inducing words are all around them? Verse 2 continues:

> The heart of the wise inclines to the right,
> but the heart of the fool to the left.
>   Even as fools walk along the road,
> they lack sense
> and show everyone how stupid they are.
>   If a ruler's anger rises against you,
> do not leave your post;
> calmness can lay great offences to rest.   (10:2–4)

We are still in the place of power, the royal court, but as we have recognised, the distribution of power is more widespread in our day and so the principles being unpacked here are relevant to all of us.

The wise man or women will have an orientation which will be different from others, having a heart which 'inclines to the right', whereas the fool 'inclines to the left' (this has nothing to do with political leanings!) and so will be different and may even be considered to be something of an odd ball and irritant because he will not just 'go with the flow'.

This is the Qoheleth's equivalent to what the New Testament writer, the apostle Paul says in his letter to the Romans, chapter 12:2, 'Do not conform any longer to the pattern of this world, but be transformed by the renewing of your mind. Then you will be able to test and approve what God's will is—his good, pleasing and perfect will.'

Paul is saying that every single person living on this planet is either being conformed or transformed. The conforming is to the 'pattern of this world', that is, a world which is in open rebellion against its Maker. It is a state which is characterised by replacing God with self at the centre of all things—it is the 'heart inclined to the left'. This is summed up by the statement of Protagoras adopted by Enlightenment thinkers that, 'Man is the measure of all things.' By way of contrast, the Christian as the follower of wisdom, is one who through a transforming of the *mind* is able to 'test and approve' what God's will is. What does that actually mean? The phrase is a translation of one word in the original, 'dokimazein.' The idea is acknowledging, proving or approving something; in this case, God's rule. It is another way of saying we will let God be God or, in the words of the Qoheleth, 'fear him and keep his commandments'. Interestingly enough, the same word is used by the apostle Paul at the beginning of Romans in chapter 1:28 where he is speaking about deviant sexual practices which he puts down to a refusal to acknowledge God in an attitude of thankfulness—'Since they did not think it worthwhile to retain the knowledge of God (same word— dokimazein) he gave them over to a depraved *mind*.' That is, he simply let them continue thinking along the paths they were already thinking—namely, thoughts which excluded God. Paul, in line with the Teacher, is saying that we are to have a different way of thinking and that comes by having God in your mind so that his values and purposes shape and transform us. It begins with seeing things differently with God at the centre of the solar system of our affections, attitudes and words, so that the glorious, resplendent reality which is *God* will exercise his gravitational pull on every piece of our lives. The consequence is that they come into their proper orbit in relation to one another and stop smashing into each other and so ruining everything. It is consciously walking through life 'under heaven'.

We may think of it like this: What would happen if our sun lost its place in the solar system? There would be interplanetary chaos. You would have Mars spinning off into endless darkness, Saturn's rings starting to crumble, Mercury might fly right into the Sun and there would be bits of the solar system strewn everywhere. It is only because they are rightly related to the Sun that it works.[113] Both Paul in Romans 1 and the writer of Ecclesiastes are saying that morally and spiritually speaking that is what has happened to humankind. God is like the sun in the solar system of our lives and if he is removed from the centre of our thinking, then our thinking and behaviour get out of control and soon the whole of society begins to collapse. What is more, it would do so entirely if not for God's grace. But when a person becomes a Christian, as he or she respond to what God has revealed, that he is a God of infinite beauty and holiness, for he is 'in heaven and we are on earth', then his infinite mass draws our thoughts to himself and things begin to come together.

While it is the case that with a renewed mind we are able to 'test and approve God's will', having a heart inclined to the right, this doesn't mean that everything will be easy—especially with those in power, in this case the king, v. 4, 'If a ruler's anger rises against you, do not leave your post; calmness can lay great offences to rest.'

The follower of wisdom will not always meet with a welcomed response, especially by those who have a vested interest and an 'agenda' which they wish to see pushed through. Sometimes these will run directly counter to what is morally right, at other times they will simply be plain foolish with a 'price tag' attached which will have to be paid for later. The temptation when facing hostility, the 'anger of the ruler', is for the believer to draw up stumps and walk away out of pique. If a decision has to be made to resign from a situation, then it is never wise to do so in a fit of temper. It is far better to allow a time of quiet reflection so that a measured and mature decision can be made. But more often than not, God simply wants us to remain calm and stay where he has placed us in life to serve him.

Topsy-turvy world

There are things worse than this, says the Qoheleth, an 'evil under the sun' when there is a complete reversal of values because there is a topsy-turvy management, v. 5:

> There is an evil I have seen under the sun,
> the sort of error that arises from a ruler:
>   Fools are put in many high positions,
> while the rich occupy the low ones.
>   I have seen slaves on horseback,
> while princes go on foot like slaves.   (10:5–7)

In the royal court the wrong people are in positions of power and privilege, while the right people the 'rich' (that is, rich in wisdom) are excluded. It leads to an absurdly frustrating situation where everything is operating in reverse, 'slaves are on horseback' while 'princes' walk about on foot.

This nightmare situation was satirised a few years ago by Mike Judge (creator of 'King of the Hill') in the science fiction comedy film, 'Idiocracy'. The film tells the story of two ordinary people from the present who take part in a top-secret military hibernation experiment, only to wake up 500 years in the future in a dystopian society full of extremely stupid people. Advertising, commercialism, and cultural anti-intellectualism have run rampant and dysgenic pressure has resulted in a uniformly dumbed-down society devoid of intellectual curiosity, social responsibility, and coherent notions of justice and human rights. This is an upside-down society where the crass and debased are considered 'cool' and valuable, while the refined and noble, characterising all truly civilised societies, are mocked and attacked.

Mike Judge's film may be extreme but it contains more than

a kernel of truth as we look around at what is happening in our society today.

We live in the celebrity culture when all that one needs to be a celebrity is to be a celebrity. This can now be secured by appearing for a few hours on 'reality TV' (a misnomer if ever there was one). It is such celebrities who are sought out for social comment, regardless of whether they have an *informed* opinion on the subject or not—what matters is mere opinion. This sells magazines and improves TV ratings. No political gathering is complete without the show biz personality to give weight to the candidate in question. We now have what William J. Donnelly calls the 'Confetti Generation':

> Having been nurtured in an Autonomy Generation, the Confetti citizen consumer will be inundated by experience and ungrounded in any cultural discipline for arriving at any reality but the self. We will witness an aggravated version of today when all ideas are equal, when all religions, life-styles, and perceptions are equally valid, equally indifferent, and equally undifferentiated in every way until given value by the choice of a specific individual. This will be the Confetti Era, when all events, ideas, and values are of the same size and weight—just pale pink and green, punched-out, die-cut wafers without distinction.[114]

If such an outlook characterises the leadership of a country or business, (or indeed a church), then disaster is just waiting to happen for folly has replaced wisdom.

Sometimes, such people and their ideas carry whole countries and cultures before them.

Back in the 1930s when National Socialism, Communism

and Western Materialism and the love of pleasure were in the ascendant, the poet; T. S. Eliot penned these words:

> But it seems that something has happened that has never happened before; though we know not just when, or why, or how, or where. Men have left God not for other gods, they say, but for no gods; and this has never happened before that both men deny gods and worship gods, professing first Reason, and then Money, and Power, and what they call Life, or Race, or Dialectic. The Church disowned, the tower overthrown, the bells upturned, what have we to do but stand with empty hands and palms upturned in an age which advances progressively backwards.[115]

With those words in mind one commentator reviewing our present situation writes: 'We live in a new dark age. Having elevated the individual as the measure of all things, modern men and women are guided solely by their own dark passions; they have nothing above themselves to respect or obey, no principles to live or die for. Personal advancement, personal feeling, and personal autonomy are the only shrines at which they worship.'[116] This is the situation when 'slaves' are elevated on horseback, and 'princes' follow on foot with heads bowed low, afraid to speak for fear of being ridiculed and disenfranchised.

Although he may be dismayed, the believer is not surprised. This is what life is like under the sun, another example of the *hebel* which characterises our world. It is into this kind of situation that the Christian can bring a Word from outside, a critical, challenging Word from God as he has revealed it in the Bible. It is also an opportunity for the church (if it has not itself surrendered to being ruled by framers of folly) to show there is a better way of living which produces works which are noble and uplifting. This has been the hallmark of the Christian church from the beginning. The Christian faith which has this view of reality under heaven has within itself the power to renew a society.

Professor Rodney Stark demonstrates how, 'Christianity served as a revitalization movement that arose in response to the misery, chaos, fear and brutality of life in the urban Greco-Roman world.' That it, 'revitalized life in Greco-Roman cities by providing new norms and kinds of social relationships able to cope with many urgent urban problems. To cities filled with the homeless and impoverished, Christianity offered charity as well as hope. To cities filled with newcomers and strangers, Christianity offered an immediate basis for attachments. To cities filled with orphans and widows, Christianity provided a new and expanded sense of family. To cities torn by violent ethnic strife, Christianity offered a new basis for social solidarity. And to cities faced with epidemics, fires and earthquakes, Christianity offered effective nursing services.'[117] The call then, as in verse 4, is for believers not to leave their posts but remain faithful and *carpe diem*—'seize the day'.

The Teacher is realistic enough, however, to realise that it is easy for people to become discouraged and downright cynical when they find themselves in such situations. Without engaging in easy triumphalism, he points to the inbuilt tendency for those who carry out such an abuse of power to eventually set themselves up for a fall which is covered by a set of parables running from verses 8–14.

Verses 8 and 9 are illustrative of these:

Whoever digs a pit may fall into it; whoever breaks through a wall may be bitten by a snake. Whoever quarries stones may be injured by them; whoever splits logs may be endangered by them.

We may think of the late President Richard Nixon who was a gifted and able man in so many ways, yet fundamentally flawed, who sought to bring down his political opponents by 'dirty tricks' only to bring himself down in ignominy in what became known as the 'Watergate Scandal'. He was not the first to find himself 'hoist by his own petard' and he won't be the last.[118]

Keep keeping on

The Qoheleth continues to be true to his name as a 'gatherer' as he collects gems of instruction to enable people to be like the Hobbit and keep on with the journey. We shall take a look at a few of these.

Verses 10–11: 'If the axe is dull and its edge unsharpened, more strength is needed, but skill will bring success. If a snake bites before it is charmed, there is no profit for the charmer.'

In the first proverb, the believer who sees the world as the Teacher sees it with 'two eyes', is to persevere under less than favourable circumstances. 'The axe is dull' and with such a poor tool it is not easy to get the job done, but that doesn't mean we give up. While the situation may be difficult it is not impossible. What is required is more effort together with increased skill. This applies to much in life which is far from ideal. 'Stickability', or what the Apostle Paul calls, 'endurance' ('hupomone'—2 Timothy 3:10) is a quality well worth cultivating.

But we are not to be naïve, especially when dealing with those in positions of authority over us; which is the point of verse 11 about the snake charmer. This takes us back to the royal court and the king who would be entertained by such a display. The word for 'charmer' is 'master of the tongue.' That is, there is a certain skill required in dealing with a person in authority who may not be acting wisely. One does not go in with 'both barrels blazing', it is important first to calm the person down so that they are in a position to hear what you have to say rather than provoking them to respond harshly with the result that we feel we have been bitten by a disturbed snake.

Fully aware of the limits of wisdom and the sad reality that folly and wickedness sometimes gain the upper hand, the Teacher is nonetheless hopeful that wisdom will win out in the end and that the way of the fool will eventually implode on itself: vv. 12–15

> Words from the mouth of the wise are gracious,
> but fools are consumed by their own lips.
> At the beginning their words are folly;
> at the end they are wicked madness—
> and fools multiply words.
> No one knows what is coming—
> who can tell someone else what will happen after them?
> The toil of fools wearies them;
> they do not know the way to town.   (10:12–15)

The point he is making is that after all the impressive words, and whatever he may possess in terms of having the 'gift of the gab', eventually the 'mover and shaker' in the court (read—government/media/academia) will show himself up as woefully inadequate, why, he is not even able to find his way back to town, let alone advise a king of the way forward!

How would you describe the mind of someone who in his autobiography had chapter headings like these: 'Why I am so intelligent.'; 'Why I write such good books'; 'Why I am Fate.' That was the father of philosophical atheism, Friedrich Nietzsche—hardly the sign of a healthy mind by any standards. A direct line can be traced from him to the person who wrote these words: 'I freed Germany from the stupid and degrading fallacies of conscience and morality … We will train young people before whom the world will tremble. I want young people capable of violence—imperious, ruthless and cruel.' That was, of course, Adolf Hitler, not exactly the model of rationality either. Tragically, in the case of Nietzsche, it was precisely madness which overcame him and he was committed to an asylum. Hitler, on the other hand, engaged in a different kind of madness by plunging humanity into the abyss of a world war. And yet in their time (and beyond) their words were considered by millions to be far from madness. A good dose of healthy realism which the Book of Ecclesiastes provides should caution us against getting too carried away by the clever communicator or the latest fad. After all, as we saw earlier, 'there is nothing new under the sun.' The wise person will be cautious.

Be bold

On the other hand, the wise person recognising the passing nature of this world and the fleeting passage of time will not be *unduly* cautious and so paralysed into inactivity. This is the balancing point made by the remaining parables of chapter 11:1–8.

> Cast your bread upon the waters, for after many days you will find it again. Give portions to seven, yes to eight, for you do not know what disaster may come upon the land.

Those living in the West will have quite a different picture in their minds to that which was originally intended. To cast 'bread upon the water' seems a senseless thing to do, unless you are feeding the ducks in the pond of the local park! All that you get with such activity is soggy bread! The original suggests something rather different, namely, that of ships laden with cargo.[119] Hence the latest NIV translation:

> Ship your grain across the sea;
> after many days you may receive a return.
>   Invest in seven ventures, yes, in eight;
> you do not know what disaster may come upon the land.

Here we have the Qoheleth balancing his earlier teaching on the need to be cautious. Exercising wisdom is not synonymous with being excessively careful, such that the man who attempts nothing achieves precisely that—nothing! As there is a time for everything (chapter 3) there is a time for taking risks. These are not necessarily wild and ill-thought-out, but a gamble nonetheless, after all, a storm might destroy the ships, sending both crew and cargo to the bottom of the sea with the investor losing everything. But life under the sun is like that. The alternative would be no achievements for fear of failure. However, having sent out your ships to trade, the return which comes back to you could be considerable, making the risk well worthwhile. There comes a time when we all have to move out of our comfort zone and attempt something great for God.

On the other hand, it may be that verse 2 is referring to the wisdom of spreading the cargo over *several* ships so that if one or two do hit trouble, then not everything would be lost.

But there may also be a secondary meaning in verse 2 relating to the need to be generous. Since seven is the complete number in the Bible, eight goes beyond that, suggesting excessive generosity. There could be more than a hint of shrewd self-interest here, the idea being that if you are generous to people when times are good for you, they hopefully will return the favour when times are bad for you. And that bad times will eventually come, often in unexpected and random ways, is illustrated by the next gems of wisdom in verses 3–8:

> If clouds are full of water,
> they pour rain on the earth.
> Whether a tree falls to the south or to the north,
> in the place where it falls, there it will lie.
> Whoever watches the wind will not plant;
> whoever looks at the clouds will not reap.
> As you do not know the path of the wind,
> or how the body is formed in a mother's womb,
> so you cannot understand the work of God,
> the Maker of all things.
> Sow your seed in the morning,
> and at evening let your hands not be idle,
> for you do not know which will succeed,

whether this or that,
or whether both will do equally well.

The societies of the West are often described as being 'secularised.'[120] Sociologists have observed that amongst the consequences of this process which pushes religion and religious ideas further and further towards the margins of public life are *rationalisation* and *disenchantment.*

Rationalisation refers to religious ideas becoming less and less meaningful and religious traditions becoming more and more marginal as other modes of thinking and traditions replace them. With the advance of modernity, God is increasingly squeezed out of the picture. So if you are ill, you call a physician not a priest; if you want good crops, you get a better fertiliser, you don't offer sacrifices to appease an angry deity.

This in turn results in what the sociologist Max Weber calls, 'disenchantment', where the 'magic' or 'mystery' of life is not just removed but unwanted; we simply apply reason and technology with the consequence that matters of faith are deemed irrelevant. The social scientist Philip Rieff sums up this modernist outlook: 'What characterises modernity, I think, is just this idea that men need not submit to any power—higher or lower—other than their own.'[121] In both cases the prevailing belief is that with the right ingenuity and technology we can happily control the future, minimise risks and bring our plans to fulfilment without the help of God thank you very much!

These sayings of the Teacher put a check on such Promethean arrogance. Whatever weather warnings we may be able to make, we still cannot prevent the downpour which can ruin crops or the hurricane which can destroy lives. If a tree falls in the forest, the direction in which it topples is a random event from our standpoint, it isn't predictable. And there is so much in life which comes under the unpredictable umbrella. And so to push the secularising mentality to the limit, waiting until we have a handle on things so we are sure of controlling the outcome of events—'watching the wind' for an opportune time to 'plant'—is likely to disappoint with the result that we end up doing very little.

There has been a massive knowledge explosion in the West during the last hundred years or so and while we now know how a baby is formed in the mother's womb (v. 5) it is still the case that we cannot understand the work of God, why tragedy should strike here and blessing there. Some things happen without any apparent rhyme or reason. God still retains his Maker's rights and is not beholden to us to give an explanation (a lesson Job had to learn the hard way—Job 38–42).

Again, this teaching does not offer an excuse for inaction on our part, on the contrary, a quiet reliance upon the Providence of God enables us to get on with whatever we turn our hands to with all the energy we can muster (9:10), sow where we can, when we can and leave the outcome to God (v. 6).

The doctrine of Providence which underlies much of the Book of Ecclesiastes is a wonderfully reassuring one. It enables the believer to make his way through the woods of life to complete the journey God has laid out for him or her. One notable believer in this doctrine, which enabled him to take risks while remaining calm and eventually dying in peace, was General Thomas 'Stonewall' Jackson.

His friend, 'Elder' Lyle once asked him if he really believed the promise that, 'All things work together for the good for those who love him, who have been called according to his purpose' (Romans 8:28). He said that he did, and so the elder asked, 'If you were to lose your health would you believe then?' 'Yes, I think I should' he replied. 'How, if you were to become entirely blind?' 'I should still believe it' replied Jackson. 'But suppose in addition to your loss of health and sight, you should become utterly dependent upon the cold charities of this world?' Jackson thought for a moment and then replied with emphasis, 'If it were the will of God to place me there, he would enable me to lie their peacefully for a hundred years.' The writer, who knew Jackson personally comments, 'He nobly stood this test when called upon to cross the Jordon River.'[122]

In the meantime what are we to do? The answer according to the Teacher is live life to the full! Verses 7–8

> Light is sweet,
> and it pleases the eyes to see the sun.
>   However many years anyone may live,
> let them enjoy them all.
> But let them remember the days of darkness,
> for there will be many.
> Everything to come is meaningless.

This is the first part of a transition poem before the narrator makes his concluding remarks in 12:8–14. The tension between affirming the 'good' amidst the 'bad and the ugly' is still retained. Life on the whole is sweet. Therefore get on and enjoy life. But this is to be set in the context of life's shadows and mist—*hebel* (v. 8b). There is the imperative to 'rejoice' (which governs verses 9–10) but balanced with the call to 'remember' (especially 12:1–7). The two go hand in hand. Rejoicing should lead to gratitude to the Giver, that is, cause us to remember him (12:1). Joy is being affirmed regardless of age. But recognising that the future is far from certain should not lead to arrogance, but a humble remembering that we are but a vapour (cf. Psalm 39:4–6) and so should set out our priorities in this light. As we have been seeing in this section, this means a healthy balance between caution and contentment on the one hand and courageousness and vision under God on the other. The 'cash value' of this approach is wonderfully set out by the writer of 'Amazing Grace', John Newton, in a letter to a friend:

(One of the marks of Christian maturity which a believer should seek is) an acquiescence in the Lord's will founded in a persuasion of his wisdom, holiness, sovereignty and goodness … So far as we attain this, we are secure from disappointment. Our own limited views, and short-sighted purposes and desires, may be, and will be, often over-ruled; but then our main and leading desire, that the will of the Lord may be done, must be accomplished. How highly does it become us, both as creatures and as sinners, to submit to the appointments of our maker! And how necessary is it to our peace! This great attainment is too often unthought-of, and over-looked; we are prone to fix our attention upon the second causes and immediate instruments of events; forgetting that whatever befalls us is according to his purpose, and therefore must be right and seasonable in itself, and shall in the issue be productive of good. From hence arise impatience, resentment, and secret repinings (i.e., complainings), which are not only sinful, but tormenting; whereas, if all things are in his hand, if the very hairs of our head are numbered; if every event, great and small, is under the direction of his providence and purpose; and if he has a wise, holy and gracious end in view, to which everything that happens is subordinate and subservient;—then we have nothing to do, but with patience and humility follow as he leads, and cheerfully to expect a happy issue … How happy are they who can resign all to him, see his hand in every dispensation, and believe that he chooses better for them than they possibly could for themselves.[123]

The Teacher could not agree more.

Questions for further thought and discussion

What is considered to be 'the way of wisdom' and 'the way of foolishness' in our age?

What examples of 'dangerous ideas' with 'sweet words' can you see in society?

Have you ever been enticed by the clever words of one who turned out to be a fool? If so what lessons have you learnt?

Think about v. 10—are there people you admire who have 'stickability' in their life under the sun?

'Life on the whole is sweet. Therefore, get on and enjoy life!' Is this the wisdom you expect to hear from the Bible? How do you enjoy life while living 'inclined to the right' (wisely) and without 'inclining to the left' (living foolishly)?

8

Age concern

Ecclesiastes 11:7–12:14

Jennifer Worth was a midwife and nurse in the East End of London in the 1950s. Her moving story has been dramatised in the award winning BBC drama series, *Call the Midwife*. She observed at first hand the whole spectrum of life 'under the sun', its exhilarating joys and despairing sorrows. In her book, *In the Midst of Life*, she reflects upon the changing social attitudes towards old age and death which have taken place in Britain during the last sixty years:

'My grandfather's death has an idealistic quality about it. His span of life had run out, he was cared for by his family, and he died peacefully in his own home. We would all wish to die like that. But, half a century later, we have to face the stark fact that for most of us it is unlikely.

Not so long ago old age was seen as the natural winding down of life, but somewhere along the way that attitude has changed. Now our waning years are viewed as a series of illnesses requiring medical intervention. A GP can prescribe drugs to arrest the symptoms of ageing, but a time will come when this is not enough and, at that stage, the elderly person is taken into hospital for treatment. This is almost compulsory these days; consequently, the majority of us will die in hospital or an institution of some sort.'

She gives a candid description of the inescapability of the ageing process:

'We who are growing old know that we are. We feel it each day in our bones, in our joints, in our balance, and our slowing down; we see it in our hair and wrinkles; we find that little things we used to do without thinking have become difficult, and the struggle gets harder as the years go by. Strength, eyesight, hearing, memory, all begin to fail us. This is ageing, and we accept it because there is no alternative. Although we try to shut it out from our minds we know that death is approaching: we "know not the day nor the hour", but we know it will come.'[124]

And yet getting older does seem to catch many unawares leaving it up to other people to remind us of what is actually happening. You go to the barber and he suggests that instead of combing you hair it might be an idea to simply rearrange it! Then there are the jokes: 'You know when you are getting older when you try to straighten out the wrinkles in your socks only to realise you aren't wearing any.' 'Forty is when you stop patting yourself on the back and start patting yourself under the chin.' Of course not everyone laughs, especially in a society like ours which is fixated with youth.

We have to admit that it is a little strange that for decades we seemed to worry about everything except getting older.

Out of all the things we couldn't count on there was one thing we could, our youth—so we thought. Those were the days when you could eat like a horse without looking like one. Life was a wide open road which stretched out endlessly before you and death? That was a millennium away. Being old and being dead happened to *other* people.

But we all know it is coming. It is not as if God has kept the ageing process a secret from us. If growing older does catch us by surprise then we certainly can't blame God for it, he has given us ample time to prepare, as well as plenty of advice. In fact, some of the most pertinent advice is found in the Book of Ecclesiastes. Interestingly enough, however, what the writer says is primarily directed to young people *before* they become old people, although what he says is also applicable to older people too as well as everyone in between.

The Teacher—'Qoheleth', is remarkably upfront about all that he considers. He does not engage in flights of fancy, he 'tells it as it is'. Therefore, he is someone we can all identify with to a greater or lesser extent. His experience is the experience of everyone living on this planet such that no matter what we do or who we are, we are left with a deep sense of frustration and incompleteness, what he calls *hebel*—'meaningless'. This is the awareness that nothing is substantial. There are so many goods in life with a dizzying variety of things to enjoy and yet we are still left with an aching void inside. Why is this? It is because God has put 'eternity into our hearts', says our writer, that is, we feel that life is meant to have purpose and direction, but we are not sure what it is. Even if we decide to give life our own meaning, that doesn't make it any more real than writing a fairy tale makes that story real. As the Teacher has made clear, such a meaning, if it exists at all, must come from 'the outside', as a gift of the Maker himself.

It is here that we come towards the climax of the Teacher's research project as he considers the climax of life—namely, death, and what often precedes it—old age. The big question to keep in mind is: in the face of death can our lives have any meaning, or is it, as Shakespeare put it, nothing but 'a tale told by an idiot full of sound and fury'? Let's find out.

When I'm sixty-four

First, the Teacher points out *the inevitability of growing* old—chapter 12:1 'Remember your Creator in the days of your youth, before the days of trouble come and the years approach when you will say, "I find no pleasure in them." Before the sun and the light and the moon and the stars grow dark, and the clouds return after the rain.'

First, there are the subtle messages of our own mortality. You are driving with a friend and they ask why you squint at all the road signs. Or maybe you are walking down the street and you notice that policemen really do look younger.

Initially, it is the odd raindrop which acts as a reminder of your passing youth and then with time the raindrops become more persistent and stronger. There comes a time when you discover that everything hurts when you wake up in the morning and what doesn't hurt, doesn't work. The actors on TV seem to mumble nowadays and you are therefore glad that there are subtitles. The smile lines don't go away when you stop smiling. Even the music of the 70s appears better than the music of today, not to mention the fashion—and that *is* serious.

But what was the occasional shower suddenly becomes a

torrent—the empty nest, the fifty candles, the bifocals, the Atkins diet. Now there is no denying it, although we try. Black hair gone grey suddenly becomes black again, or better still, blond. Wrinkles disappear and the skin becomes shiny courtesy of Botox. The family estate car is traded in for a white sports car and for a while we delude ourselves that the ageing process has been put on hold. But the calendar pages still turn, the clock steadily ticks and time relentlessly marches on and there is no escaping it, as the writer says, 'the clouds return after the rain.' The plain fact is that we are not going to wake up one morning and suddenly find ourselves young again. While we may feel as if we are still a thirty-year old something on the inside, the outside of our body painfully reminds us (often literally) that we are not.

This is the way our writer describes the *effects of growing old*—v:3–5

> when the keepers of the house tremble, and the strong men stoop, when the grinders cease because they are few, and those looking through the windows grow dim; when the doors to the street are closed and the sound of grinding fades; when men rise up at the sound of birds, but all their songs grow faint; when men are afraid of heights and of dangers in the streets; when the almond tree blossoms and the grasshopper drags himself along and desire no longer is stirred. Then man goes to his eternal home and mourners go about the streets.

This is a highly imaginative way of describing what eventually happens to us with the passage of time as it operates at two levels; the literal and the metaphorical.

At the literal level, it is the case that even strong men, like the athletes the world idolises at the Olympics, eventually begin to stoop. The days of having a 'lie in' on a Saturday morning are gone, because no matter how hard you try you can't help but wake up early to the sound of the dawn chorus, except that because of your failing hearing the sound gets fainter and fainter until you can't hear anything at all without the assistance of a cochlea implant! What is more disturbing perhaps, is the increasing sense of vulnerability and nervousness we feel as we get older, so that climbing ladders becomes a scary business—'men are afraid of heights.' And it does seem rather unwise to venture out on your own onto the street at night because who knows—you might get mugged or have an accident—there are 'dangers in the street'. Nor does it end there, for even the libido, our sexual appetite is affected, 'desire is no longer stirred.' All perfectly natural says our writer and all part of the frustrations of life—*hebel.*

However, at the same time we have metaphorical language being employed to describe what takes place with ageing as the body is likened to a house falling into disrepair. There are the 'keepers of the house trembling', referring to the arms as they are no longer as strong as they once were; you try and lift a weight and they shake with the strain. The 'strong men stooping' conceivably refers to the legs. The 'grinders' denote teeth, they begin to fall out or disintegrate. Those 'looking through windows growing dim' are the eyes—we all need spectacles eventually. The 'almond tree blossoming' represents the hair turning white whilst 'the grasshopper dragging himself along' is a picture of ungainly walking, as we shuffle along the floor. We no longer conduct ourselves with a spring in our step but with a frame in our hands. Time, they say 'is a great healer but a lousy beautician'. But where is all of this heading? The answer is death—v. 6 'Remember him(that is God) before the silver cord is severed, or the golden bowl is broken; before the pitcher is shattered at the spring, or the wheel broken at the well, and the dust returns to the ground it came from, and the spirit returns to God who gave it.'

Life is portrayed as a slender 'silver cord' to which is attached a golden bowl. When this is severed by death the bowl simply falls to the ground, rolling around empty until it comes to rest. Or life might be thought of as being like a pitcher which is lowered into a well by a pulley. The pitcher is shattered when the wheel is broken by death so that the waters of life can no longer be renewed. That is where we are all heading. The writer gives us a clue as to why this is so in v. 7, 'the dust returns to the ground it came from' (cf. 3:20).

Here is an allusion to Genesis chapter 3 and God's judgement upon our rebellion against him, 'By the sweat of your brow you will eat your food until you return to the ground, since from it you were taken; for dust you are and to dust you will return.' (v. 19). From beginning to end the Bible tells us that we were made for a relationship with God and it is in this we were meant to find meaning and satisfaction. The beauty and bliss of this relationship is wonderfully depicted in the second chapter of Genesis as the man and the woman as God's representatives in the garden enjoy open access into God's presence as he freely addresses them and walks amongst them. It is a wistful picture of harmony and openness. But that is a relationship we no longer enjoy, for like Adam we each have decided to go our own way and sever that relationship and this always brings in its wake judgement in terms of dissatisfaction and ultimately death—the most poignant and inescapable reminder that all is not well between ourselves and our Maker. Death symbolises the accumulation of evil, sorrow, suffering and despair which the spiritual and moral infection of sin brings in its train.

In his treatise the writer of Ecclesiastes undertakes a wide ranging survey of a world on the run from God—a world where chaos mingles with order, vice with virtue, ugliness with beauty, death with life. This is *our* world he is describing and our experience. His conclusion: v. 8 'Meaningless, meaningless, everything is meaningless.' So what are we to do in the face of this feeling of emptiness and ultimately death?

To answer that question we turn to *the response to growing old*. In fact, it might better be described as *the response to living* and it is there in verse 1 and verse 6—it is to *remember,* 'Remember your Creator'. What that involves is unpacked for us by the 'frame narrator' in v. 13, 'Now all has been heard: here is the conclusion of the matter: Fear God and keep his commandments for this is the whole duty of man' 'Why?' 'For God will bring every deed into judgement including every hidden thing, whether good or evil.'

Drawing upon everything the Teacher has been saying, which from the standpoint of living 'under the sun', the conclusion is that everything feels ultimately pointless. Our significance on this tiny, tiny planet, in a galaxy of a billion stars, with a billion other galaxies in a vast impersonal universe is of *no* more consequence at all—*if* that is all there is. How can it? But our writer knows that there *is* more; that there is 'the Creator' and knowing that makes all the difference in the world. Let me explain how.

Only *created* things can have meaning. By way of an illustration, think of a microphone. What meaning does it have? In and of itself it has no meaning. The meaning it has is what its creator, owner and judge give it (of course one person might fulfil all these roles). Whoever made it did so with a purpose in mind, namely, to pick up a voice or sound which, once fed into an amplifier and speaker, projects that sound. The creator gave it that meaning or purpose, if you will. But once it has been sold the *owner* can, if he wanted to, give it a different meaning. For example, the owner could take it and stir a bucket of wallpaper paste with it or use it as cosh. Those may be odd uses to be sure (abuses some might say), but meaningful uses nonetheless. But one day its judge will give it meaning too and evaluate it by maybe declaring, 'This is a useless microphone, it no longer works and so I am going to throw it in the bin.' Or, he may say, 'This is a great microphone; I am going to buy another one just like it.' The Maker of it, the Owner of it and the Judge of it—all give it meaning. But just supposing that the microphone, in some Disneyesque way, could be given consciousness together with a voice, it could not give itself meaning—for instance, by declaring itself to be an item for eating. So it is with us. We are not 'plastic people' able to change shape and significance at will. There are constraints imposed upon us by virtue of being constituted in a certain way for a specific purpose. The liberating message of the Teacher is we don't have to try, for we do have a Maker, Owner and Judge in God. Our meaning and significance is derived from our relationship with him which lies behind the word 'fear' or 'awe' (v. 13), for this is part of the proper response of the creature to the Creator, who is to be worshipped and obeyed. Since he is the one who designed us he knows how we best function, and since he has given us his commands in the Bible, following those wisely means we can live meaningful lives, lives of love for God and for each other.

When we were young

If it is the case, as the Teacher's experience and our own confirms, that we are out of sorts with our Creator and so not properly aligned to the world such that things keep jarring, how are we going to get back in touch with him? The message of the New Testament to which this book points is that the Maker has got in touch with us in the person of Jesus Christ, 'The Teacher and King of Israel, *Son of David.*' Indeed, Matthew emphasises this connection right at the beginning of his biography of Jesus as he 'tops and tails' Jesus' family tree, 'A record of the genealogy of Jesus Christ the *Son of David*' (v. 1), 'of whom was born Jesus, who is called Christ (Messiah)', (v. 16).

Notice how the writer urges us to get things sorted out while we are young, 11:9,

> Be happy, young man, while you are young, and let your heart give you joy in the days of your youth. Follow the ways of your heart and whatever your eyes see, but know that for all these things God will bring you to judgement.

The most productive time in our lives, when we have energy, idealism and vigour is in our twenties and thirties. Any time is a good time to become reconnected with God by becoming a Christian, but *especially* when you are young, for then you can make your life really count for something and enjoy life as it is meant to be enjoyed because you know what life is all about. You are able to see that food and drink and friendships and clothes and a whole host of things, have not just appeared out of nowhere, but are wonderful gifts coming from the hands of the great Giver who is known personally to us as a heavenly Father. You can use your youth and energy not just being a couch potato stuck in front of the box—X-box or TV box, but getting out and about in sharing the Gospel with others and using whatever talents you have in serving God and his people.

It is at this point that we can make a serious misjudgement and think that it is possible to live a hedonistic life now and put off becoming a Christian until much later on, perhaps when you are old or even lying on your death bed. However, a moment's pause will help to see how wrongheaded this kind of reasoning is. For a start, it assumes you are going to have time to prepare for your death which is not necessarily the case. Accidents happen, terminal illnesses are contracted without warning. What is more, if you do die in old age in hospital, as Jennifer Worth says is increasingly likely for us all, you may be so drugged up to the eyeballs you probably won't have a clue as to what is going on anyway! No, our writer is insistent, *now* is the time to get right with your Maker and make something of your life which eventually is going to be judged. And we are to thank God that it is so, for that judgement will give meaning to our life.

Now we are old

But what of those who are getting older, how are they to spend what little time is left on earth?

Let me say that there are two wrong responses and one right response.

The first wrong turn we can take is to give in to *regret*. The feeling can be suffocating. It could be that you have given the best years of your life to the company and at the end of it the mahogany desk is left feeling cold, the obligatory retirement watch seems so meagre and our achievements so hollow. This is the 'meaningless' of Ecclesiastes. You look around for lasting satisfaction in what you have done but it is nowhere to be found. The result is that we wallow in regret while chanting the mantra: 'If only ...' 'If only I had worked harder at school.' 'If only I had not worked every hour God sent and missed the children growing up.' 'If only I had pursued a career and forgot about a family' 'If only.'

This kind of tragedy is captured by the song, *The Cat's in the Cradle*:

A child arrived just the other day,
He came to the world in the usual way.
But there were planes to catch, and bills to pay.
He learned to walk while I was away.
And he was talking 'fore I knew it, and as he grew,
He'd say, 'I'm gonna be like you, Dad.
You know I'm gonna be like you.'
And the cat's in the cradle and the silver spoon,
Little boy blue and the man in the moon.
'When you coming home, Dad?' 'I don't know when,
But we'll get together then.
You know we'll have a good time then.'
My son turned ten just the other day.
He said, 'Thanks for the ball, dad, come on let's play.
Can you teach me to throw?' I said, 'Not today,
I got a lot to do.' He said, 'That's ok.'
And he walked away, but his smile never dimmed,

Said, 'I'm gonna be like him, yeah.
You know I'm gonna be like him.'
And the cat's in the cradle and the silver spoon,
Little boy blue and the man in the moon.
'When you coming home, Dad?' 'I don't know when,
But we'll get together then.
You know we'll have a good time then.'
Well, he came from college just the other day,
So much like a man I just had to say,
'Son, I'm proud of you. Can you sit for a while?'
He shook his head, and he said with a smile,
'What I'd really like, Dad, is to borrow the car keys.
See you later. Can I have them please?'
And the cat's in the cradle and the silver spoon,
Little boy blue and the man in the moon.
'When you coming home, son?' 'I don't know when,
But we'll get together then, Dad.
You know we'll have a good time then.'
I've long since retired and my son's moved away.
I called him up just the other day.
I said, 'I'd like to see you if you don't mind.'
He said, 'I'd love to, dad, if I could find the time.
You see, my new job's a hassle, and the kid's got the flu,
But it's sure nice talking to you, dad.
It's been sure nice talking to you.'
And as I hung up the phone, it occurred to me,
He'd grown up just like me.
My boy was just like me.

The real tragedy of that song resides in the life of the man
who recorded it, Harry Chapin. His wife who wrote the

lyrics asked him one day when he was going to slow down his frantic pace of life and give some time to his children. His answer was: 'At the end of this busy summer, I'll take some time to be with them then.' That summer, Harry Chapin was killed in a car accident.

Secondly, there is *rebellion:* rebellion against the demands, rebellion against the mundane. As a consequence you turn against your job, your church, even your family.

This is when the mid-life crisis opens up into one of the devil's oldest traps—adultery. There is the pretty young secretary who not only brings you a heap of papers but a whole heap of sympathy ... Then there is the man next door who simply can't believe that you have had four children and still keep your figure so trim ... The scene has been played out many times before and no doubt will be played out time and time again.

Therefore an attempt to retrieve some sort of significance out of our lives is made by a desperate rekindling of youthful passions as we begin to flatter ourselves—'There is still life in the old boy yet' only to deceive ourselves—'It's only a bit of fun'; until eventually we hurt ourselves—and others. Make no mistake, the fruits of such rebellion are very short lived and regret comes back to haunt us with a vengeance. There is guilt associated with the family you have abandoned and the vows you have broken. There is the suspicion which hangs in the air of the new relationship—for if he or she has betrayed once, who is to say they will not do it again, and again and again? Misery is added to misery, but that is not the way the romantic paperbacks or Hollywood will portray it. The grass may look greener on the other side of the fence, but the moment you step onto it, it becomes scorched earth.

The better way brings us back full circle to the concluding verses 13 and 14, 'Now all has been heard: here is the conclusion of the matter: Fear God and keep his commandments for this is the whole duty of man' 'Why?' 'For God will bring every deed into judgement including every hidden thing, whether good or evil.' [125]

Contrary to what the media in particular and society at large may tell us (and indeed our own feelings as we have followed the Teacher at points); we are not nothings, coming from nowhere and going nowhere and so are free to do our own thing. We are responsible beings made by a good and caring Creator to whom we are to give an account for the way we have lived our lives.

One of the things which contributes to our sense of drivenness is that many have lost any sense that our lives constitute a story, a purposeful narrative so that what matters is what we make of our lives, having them being given shape and direction by who we are and what we do. For many today life tends to be fragmented, with little awareness of the past and little concern for the future. One of the dominant features of postmodernism is the lack of what is called a 'meta-narrative', an overall, overarching story which gives meaning to who we are and what we do. The result is that we live for the moment, filling our lives with activities like an alcoholic filling his stomach with drink. The existentialist philosopher, Martin Heidegger, called this presumption in the way we view the present as 'the proudly Exclusive Now' or indeed, as 'the strutting point.'

But the writer of Ecclesiastes would have us reconsider such a standpoint given that we do have a Creator. Indeed it might be helpful to imagine that what we are all doing with our lives is writing a story, a story which is to be read by God and judged by him. How do you want your life story to look? More to the point, how do you want your *final* chapters to read? Simply as a catalogue of complaints, a list of vain regrets, something shameful which you really would not want your children or grandchildren to view, let alone God? There is no reason for the final chapters of our lives not to be some of the grandest chapters.

Think about others who have done just that.

Winston Churchill was 66 years old when he became Prime Minister in 1940 and embarked upon his greatest achievement. He was 79 years old when he was awarded the Nobel Prize for literature.

A friend of the famous American jurist Oliver Wendell Holmes asked him why he had taken up the study of Greek at the age of 94. He replied, 'Well, my good sir, it is now or never.'

After Michelangelo died, someone found in his studio a note written to himself which read: 'Draw Antonio, draw, and do not waste time.' Times slips away. Days pass. Years fade. And life comes to an end. What God wants us to do while there is time we are to do. Here is a helpful observation from Lewis Smedes about the importance of pausing to ponder:

'Most of us spend our time crawling, groping, climbing, sometimes running, but always moving like the works of a clock. But now and then joy comes to arrest the motion, it stops the tedious ticking of our life-clocks with the bracing discovery that we have received a gift. It works most magnificently when we feel our own life as if it were God's gift to us.'[126]

The Teacher would affirm that with a hearty 'Amen'

While our society may be 'ageist' our Creator most decidedly is not. God's oldest have been amongst his choicest since their characters have been finely honed by time and experience as they have taken to heart the exhortation of the closing words of Ecclesiastes—'fear God and keep his commandments'.

Think of Moses, who, when over 80 led the people out of Egypt, was much more effective than the young prince of Egypt in his 20s. Or Anna who was an eighty-five-year-old widow who, although having failing eyesight, had enough vision to recognise the infant Messiah when he came. Think too of the apostle John. Maybe *we* would have thought he had achieved his life's work having penned his Gospel, but not God. There still had to come the Book of Revelation, written when he was probably well into his 90s.

Maybe God intends the same with you and me, perhaps not as striking as some of those just mentioned but just as significant from God's point of view. Getting older doesn't mean that our sense of adventure has to correspondingly diminish. Instead of building a fire in our hearth maybe we should ask God to build a fire in our heart.

Questions for further thought and discussion
What emotions come to mind when you think about getting old?

Questions for the younger:
How do you want your 'life story' to look?

In what areas of your life do you need to resist the temptation to 'live for the Executive Now'?

What patterns and habits can you put into practice now that will help you live your life 'under Heaven', with the return and judgement of Christ in view?

Questions for the older:

How do you want your 'final chapter' to look?

What feelings of regret do you harbour and in what ways are you tempted to rebel against your ageing?

How does the call to 'fear God and keep his commandments' transform how you deal with these attitudes and approach the rest of your life?

If you're not sure which category you fall into, do both!

9

Life under the Son

Here is part of a song written by Sydney Carter, who is better known for the hymn, *Lord of the Dance*:

It was on a Friday morning that they took me from the cell
and I saw they had a carpenter to crucify as well
You can blame it on to Pilate
You can blame it on the Jews
You can blame it on the Devil
It's God I accuse
It's God they ought to crucify instead of you and me
I said to the carpenter, a-hanging on the tree
Now Barabbas was a killer
And they let Barabbas go
But you are being crucified
For nothing that I know
And your God is up in Heaven
and He doesn't do a thing

With a million angels watching
and they never move a wing
It's God they ought to crucify instead of you and me
I said to the carpenter, a-hanging on the tree

It would be fair to say there are many people today who would echo those sentiments. As they look upon the pain and misery which is so rampant in the world, the cry goes out, 'Why does God allow it to happen? It may be all right for him cocooned from such afflictions in the comfort of heaven, but what about his creatures down here on earth? God hasn't a clue as to what it is like to live and die in a broken world such as ours.'

Certainly the brokenness of the world 'East of Eden' has been pondered to great depths by the Teacher and for him God does seem rather remote, after all, 'God is in heaven' (5:2). But this does not mean that God is not involved at all or carrying out his purposes. All of life and the 'goods' of life are a personal gift of God (3:13); he tests men (3:18); he lays on their hearts the awareness of eternity (3:11) and will judge (3:17). This is no Deistic deity who has set the universe in motion and excused himself from its running and so abdicated responsibility for what he has made.

Nonetheless, the charge of the songwriter does echo perhaps more stridently the voice of the Qoheleth with the words, 'God is up in heaven and he doesn't do a thing'. But if that is so, the underlying sentiment must be taken together with the sense that there is much more to be had in the future, 'God will bring every deed to judgement'—there is a future dimension yet to be realised.

The New Testament writers taking their cue from Jesus

himself, see that in different ways the various parts of the Old
Testament within the gradual unfolding plan of God, point
to, and find their fulfilment in, the Lord Jesus Christ: 'In the
past God spoke to our forefathers through the prophets at
various times and in various ways (this includes Ecclesiastes),
but in these last days he has spoken to us by his Son, whom
he has appointed heir of all things.' (Hebrews 1:1). Similarly,
Jesus construes his own identity and mission in similar terms,
'Beginning with Moses and all the Prophets, he explained to
them what was said in *all* the Scriptures concerning himself.'
(Luke 24:27).

How does the Teacher and the teachings of Ecclesiastes
relate to the one who in the Gospels is frequently referred to
as 'Teacher' (e.g. John 11:8), who by his own self-designation
is described as 'greater than Solomon' (Matthew 12:42)? In
other words, what was it like for 'the Son' to live 'under the
sun' and what are its implications for us?

A time to be born

The Christian faith is the most exciting drama that ever
staggered the imagination of man … the plot pivots on a
single character, and the whole action is the answer to a single
central problem—What do you think of Christ? The Church's
answer is categorical and uncompromising, and it is this: That
Jesus Bar-Joseph, the carpenter of Nazareth, was in fact and in
truth … the God by whom all things were made. His body and
brain were those of a common man; his personality was the
personality of God … He was not a kind of demon pretending
to be human; he was in every respect a genuine living man. He
was not merely a man so good as to be 'like God'—he was God.
This is the dogma we find so dull—this is the terrifying drama

of which God is both victim and hero. If this is dull, then what in Heaven's name is worthy to be called exciting? The people who hanged Christ never accused him of being a bore—on the contrary they thought him too dynamic to be safe. It has been left to later generations to muffle up that shattering personality and surround him with an atmosphere of tedium. We have efficiently pared the claws of the Lion of Judah, certified him 'meek and mild', and recommended him as a fitting household pet for pale curates and pious old ladies. To those who knew him, however, he no way suggests a milk-and-water person; they objected to him as a dangerous firebrand … He was emphatically not a dull man in his human lifetime, and if he was God, there can be nothing dull about God either.

So writes Dorothy L. Sayers.[127] Sayers highlights the breath-taking claim which is unique to the Christian faith—God became man.

At the beginning of his startling biography of Jesus, the apostle John unpacks this claim in terms of the arrival of 'the Word' (the Logos):

> In the beginning was the Word, and the Word was with God, and the Word was God. He was with God in the beginning. Through him all things were made; without him nothing was made that has been made. In him was life, and that life was the light of all mankind. (John 1:1–4)

And what did this 'Word', the self-expression of God who is God, do? John tells us a few verses later (v. 14): 'The Word became flesh and made his dwelling among us. We have seen his glory, the glory of the one and only Son, who came from the Father, full of grace and truth.'

That is, using the language of Ecclesiastes, the Son was born 'under the sun'. Divinity had arrived in human form. This happened in a specific locatable place at a specific datable time. Heaven opened herself and placed her most precious being into the uterus of a teenage Jewish girl called Mary. The Omnipotent, in one instant, made himself breakable. The One who had been Spirit from all eternity became pierceable. When John says, 'The Word became flesh' he means that God became a foetus. He was given eyebrows, elbows, two kidneys, and a spleen. He stretched against the walls and floated in the amniotic fluids of his mother. He was, while being completely divine, completely human. Apart from growing, what was the 'Word' doing while he was moving around in that womb? He was actually upholding the universe. This is how one early Christian thinker, Athanasius, put it:

> The Word was not hedged in by His body, nor did His presence in the body prevent His being present elsewhere as well … At one and the same time—this is the wonder—as Man he was living a human life, and as Word he was sustaining the life of the Universe, and as Son He was in constant union with the Father.[128]

It is worth pondering this amazing claim if we are going to feel the impact that it is God as a man who experienced for a while life as *hebel*—mist.

Consider these words of another Christian writer of the 5th century, Augustine,

He (Jesus), through whom time was made, was made in time; and He, older by eternity than the world itself, was younger in age than many of His servants in the world; He, who made man, was made man; He was given existence by a mother whom He brought into existence; He was carried in hands which He formed; He nursed at breasts which He filled; He cried like a babe in the manger in speechless infancy——this Word without which human eloquence is speechless![129]

What a magnificent description! The 16th century writer, John Calvin, wrestling with the same idea, puts it this way:

Even if the Word in his immeasurable essence united with the nature of man into one person, we do not imagine that he was confined therein. Here is something marvellous: the Son of God descended from heaven in such a way that, without leaving heaven, he willed to be borne in the virgin's womb, to go about the earth, and to hang upon the cross; yet he continuously filled the world even as he had done from the beginning.[130]

Let's just try and get our minds around some of the implications of this doctrine. This belief means that the little baby born in Nazareth was sustaining the sun which is a star a million times the size of the earth and one the other 100 billion stars which make up the Milky Way galaxy together with the other 100 billion galaxies dispersed throughout the universe; that the one who lay in the wooden manger was the one whose genius and power brought into being the mighty trees out of which that little box was made. It means that as a young man pinned helplessly to a cross it was only by his sovereign will as King of the Universe that the atoms of those nails kept their structure so that the nails remained in place tearing into his flesh. While still a human being his glorious presence was such that he fills the whole cosmos so that he is there at the birth of a supernova in some remote corner of the galaxy, transcending space and time while inhabiting space and time in a dusty, despised corner of the Roman Empire. Remember what the Teacher says about man trying to get a handle on God's ways? 'They cannot fathom what God has done from beginning to end.' (3:11). Too true, especially when thinking of the Incarnation!

But without compromising his divinity, God the Son became fully human, 'born of the virgin Mary' as the Christian creeds would have it.

Has it ever crossed your mind that God could have arrived in our world in all sorts of other ways; maybe by beaming down from heaven like some extra-terrestrial in Star Trek? Why choose this method which is so sticky, messy and gross? The answer is that it was to ensure his humanity. One of the things that make us human is our family history. We all have a family tree and each family tree is connected to all other family trees in the world so giving solidarity to what is called the *human* race. Without an ancestry you are not human and both Luke and Matthew underscore Jesus' humanity by tracing out his ancestry. What is more, what makes us the persons we are is not just the specific combination of genes or our upbringing in the home but, as research increasingly suggests, what happens to us while we are developing in the womb—that shapes our character too. Therefore, if God is to become human, sharing our pains, stresses, and joys, then he must become human from the very point we all become human—namely at conception. The claim of the Bible is that Jesus is *physically* connected to the Qoheleth, for he too is a descendant of David.

A time to weep and a time to laugh

The humanity of Jesus ensures he is one with us in our emotional life.

The intense emotional life that Jesus shared with the rest of us 'under the sun', is focused for us by Mark in his biographical account of the life of Jesus (in fact the descriptions are so colourful and detailed that they can only be accounts of eyewitnesses and so vouchsafing their historical reliability).[131]

It is Mark who records how Jesus seeing the crowd of followers in the desert was 'moved with compassion' (Mark 6:34). He is the one who, in the account of Jesus healing the deaf mute in Mark 7:31–37, relates Jesus, 'Looking up to heaven and with a deep sigh (*estenaxen*) said "Be opened"'. Why the sigh? It might well be because Jesus is feeling precisely what the Qoheleth felt many years before him, the deep sense of frustration with the afterbirth of the effects of sin in the creation—'the normal abnormality' which characterises the *hebel* of this life. This is not mere speculation because the same verb is used by the Apostle Paul in Romans 8 as he gives a description of creation which is very much in line with that of the Teacher, 'For the creation was subject to frustration (or futility—*mataiotes*—the same word used by the Greek translation of the Bible known as the Septuagint (LXX) to translate *hebel* in Ecclesiastes)'. Then verse 22, 'We know that the whole creation has been groaning (*systenazei*—a similar word, which has the same root, to that used to describe Jesus' sighing in Mark) as in the pains of childbirth.' In this passage Paul shares the outlook of the Qoheleth regarding the experience of the world as frustrated and frustrating as part of the fall-out of the brokenness of our world. Jesus is confronted by that brokenness and in his person and ministry begins to reverse the debilitating effects of sin.

Another account, this time from John's Gospel, which lifts the veil on Jesus' emotional life as he comes face to face with the ultimate leveller and cause of futility—death, is found in the moving episode of the raising of Lazarus in John 11. Here we see that for Jesus there is not only a time to weep but a time to be angry.

We read of Jesus deliberately arriving at the tomb late. Lazarus, the brother of the two sisters Martha and Mary, had been dead for four days and so his body would have started to undergo decay (John 11:39). On his way to the grief stricken home Jesus is met by Mary and we are told, 'When Jesus saw her weeping, and the Jews who had come along with her also weeping (they were professional mourners), he was *deeply moved in spirit and troubled.*' (v. 33). Then we have the shortest description of Jesus ever recorded, it simply says, 'Jesus wept' (v. 35). The verb translated, 'deeply moved in spirit' is a very strong one; it could rightly be translated 'outraged' (*embrimaomai*—literally 'to snort in spirit' like a wild horse). Why should Jesus feel such rage at this point? It couldn't have been the sort of grief or anger we might feel at a funeral—the anger of loss, because he knew what he was about to do, namely, raise Lazarus from the dead. Surely, the answer is that he is angry with *death itself.* He sees the loss and pain it causes. Entering his Father's world as the Son of God, he found not the order and beauty of his Father's original creation, but fractured disorder, raw ugliness, and complete disarray—everywhere the shattered world gone bad because of sin. Standing at that graveside he was confronted with a death of someone he loved which symbolised the accumulation of all the evil, sorrow, suffering and despair which the moral infection of sin introduces—and he is angry. 'As one dies, so dies another. All have the same breath; man has no advantage over the animal. Everything is vapour. All go to the same place; all come from dust, and to dust all return' (Ecclesiastes 3:19–20, echoing the curse of Genesis 3:19 alluded to by Paul in Romans 8). But this is not a hard callous rage; this is compassionate anger for he also weeps. There is a time to weep—and God wept!

There is, however, a time to laugh

This was recognised by Jesus and was considered by him to be proverbial. For example, at one time his disciples were being criticised for not fasting in the tradition of the Pharisees and John the Baptist's followers, and in order to defend them (and by implication himself), he replied, 'How can the guests of the bridegroom fast while he is with them? They cannot, so long as they have him with them. But the time will come when the bridegroom will be taken from them, and on that day they will fast.' (Mark 2:19–20).[132]

Joy especially celebrated through eating and drinking, is a major theme in Ecclesiastes. It is in part an expression of *shalom*, the wholesome peaceful relationship which is had with God and others. It is 'to enjoy living before God, to enjoy living in one's physical surroundings, to enjoy living with one's fellows, to enjoy life with oneself.'[133]

Such enjoyment was positively encouraged by the Qoheleth (2:24–28; 3:13; 5:18–20; 9:7–10).[134] Jesus by his actions, as well as by his teaching, affirms this. But Jesus is moving things on even further. Whereas for the Qoheleth such joy in eating and drinking took place in the shadow of death which made life feel futile, Jesus is in the business of restoring things, bringing about that *shalom* which characterises the Kingdom of God and replaces the futile with the substantial. By placing an emphasis on feasting (especially with the outcasts for which he was roundly criticised by the religious establishment—Luke 5:30; 15:1) Jesus was pointing to the future time anticipated by the prophet Isaiah, the moment when everything will be restored and death and tears will be no more. The feasting of Jesus' ministry is a foretaste of the great Messianic banquet yet to come (Matthew 8:11).

It is therefore not surprising that joy and feasting were such prominent features in the life and ministry of Jesus.[135] Indeed, there is more than a note of irony in one of the most famous and moving parables Jesus ever told, 'The Parable of the Prodigal Son'. This was spoken not only to defend his practice of 'eating with tax collectors and sinners', but to point to what he had come to earth in order to achieve; the overcoming of the 'vaporising' effect of sin in God's world which so troubled the Qoheleth and which so vexes us.

The parable reaches its climax with the return of the Prodigal which resulted in feasting and dancing, a party to which the begrudging elder brother (representing Jesus' critics) is invited:

But while he was still a long way off, his father saw him and was filled with compassion for him; he ran to his son, threw his arms around him and kissed him.

The son said to him, 'Father, I have sinned against heaven and against you. I am no longer worthy to be called your son.'

But the father said to his servants, 'Quick! Bring the best robe and put it on him. Put a ring on his finger and sandals on his feet. Bring the fattened calf and kill it. Let's have a feast and celebrate. For this son of mine was dead and is alive again; he was lost and is found.' So they began to celebrate.

Meanwhile, the older son was in the field. When he came near the house, he heard music and dancing. So he called one of the servants and asked him what was going on. 'Your brother has come,' he replied, 'and your father has killed the fattened calf because he has him back safe and sound.'

The older brother became angry and refused to go in. So his father went out and pleaded with him. But he answered his father, 'Look! All these years I've been slaving for you and never disobeyed your orders. Yet you never gave me even a young goat so I could celebrate with my friends. But when this son of yours who has squandered your property with prostitutes comes home, you kill the fattened calf for him!'

'My son,' the father said, 'you are always with me, and everything I have is yours. But we had to celebrate and be glad, because this brother of yours was dead and is alive again; he was lost and is found.'   (Luke 15:20–32)

There is a Divine 'must' about rejoicing in God's Kingdom. Jesus was steeped in the Old Testament Scriptures; they constituted God's Word which 'could not be broken.'[136] They all pointed to him. The Book of Ecclesiastes would itself have been a major source from which he would have taken his understanding of God's kingdom.[137] What was lost because of the fall begins to be restored by Jesus in order that all life should be brought under 'the heavens' by the one who did 'fear God and keep his commands' on our behalf.[138]

As we saw in chapter 3, various experiences and encounters we have in life are meant to act as 'signals of transcendence' or 'footprints' of the Maker, creating within us a sense of well-being on the one hand and frustration on the other. This is certainly the case with joy and the times 'to laugh' and 'dance'. Not only did the meals Jesus provide a foretaste of what can be had with God now through his Son and what is to come in the 'new heavens and new earth', but they also provide windows into the nature of God himself.

This was something the former atheist turned Christian proponent, C. S. Lewis, discovered. C. S. Lewis entitled his spiritual biography *Surprised by Joy*. He speaks of the climax of discovering this joy:

> No slightest hint vouchsafed me that there ever had been or ever would be any connection between God and Joy. If anything, it was the reverse. I had hoped that the heart of reality might be such a kind that we can symbolise it as a place; instead I found it to be a Person.[139]

Joy is a person!

Every human being in one way or another is looking for joy or happiness. This is what the Qoheleth has been arguing. This is the way we are wired. At various points along the way we have glimpses of joy: the joy found in the company of a friend around a meal, the joy at the birth of a baby, the joy of savouring a beautiful sunset, and yet these are not Joy itself—the product, but simply the by-product. They are not the flower, they are the scent. The reality is to be found elsewhere in a Person and the person's name is Jesus.

Joy was not only one of the great hallmarks of Jesus' ministry, but his character. It was this joy he promised to give his followers, 'These things I have spoken to you, that *my* joy may be in you, and that your joy may be full,' (John 15:11). Has it ever struck you that Jesus was the happiest man who ever lived? Despite all the injustices thrown at him and all the disappointments which surrounded him, not once do you detect in Jesus even a hint of self-pity. More than that, when, for instance, he sent his disciples out on a mission to announce the inbreaking of God's kingdom into this world of vapour, we find this amazing description of Jesus' reaction to their return in Luke's Gospel, 'At that time Jesus, full of joy through the Holy Spirit, said "I praise you Father, the Lord of heaven and earth."'(Luke 10:21). Here we are given a tantalizing glimpse into the life of the God who is the 'family' of Trinity, and we see scintillating joy. The Holy Spirit is the mediator of joy to the Son from the Father, and the Son expresses delight to the Father in praise. So this means before there was a universe to enjoy, there *was* Joy—the sheer, enraptured delight of the Father for the Son, the Son's joy in the Father, shared between them by the mediating Person of the Holy Spirit who is Joy.[140] Yes, the Qoheleth was onto something very important and Jesus came to bring it—joy.

A time to die

But for the Teacher, all human happiness which is rooted in relationships is passing; this too is *hebel*, a chasing after the wind. This is primarily because of death which casts its long dark shadow on all the 'goods' of God's world. In fact, even the vision of God's kingdom which Jesus in part expressed in his celebratory meals—the times of laughing and dancing, also highlight the brokenness and contradictions which we experience in this life. Death, therefore, must be dealt with if lasting *shalom* is to be achieved.

And so we come to the ultimate identification of God with the world of *hebel* the surrendering of his life to death.

As we have seen, through the healings of Jesus and especially the bringing back to life of Lazarus, we are given glimpses of what Jesus came to achieve as the one who is 'The Resurrection and the Life' (11:25).

We have also noted how the writer of Ecclesiastes does not so much argue a case as to invite his readers to follow him on a journey. The Apostle Paul does something very similar as he considers the journey of God the Son into this world of mist and vapour and finally death in Philippians 2:5

In your relationships with one another, have the same attitude
as Christ Jesus:
Who, being in very nature God,
did not consider equality with God something to be used to his
own advantage;
rather, he made himself nothing
by taking the very nature of a servant,
being made in human likeness.
And being found in appearance as a man,
he humbled himself
by becoming obedient to death—
even death on a cross!

> Therefore God exalted him to the highest place
> and gave him the name that is above every name,
> that at the name of Jesus every knee should bow,
> in heaven and on earth and under the earth,
> and every tongue acknowledge that Jesus Christ is Lord,
> to the glory of God the Father.

The centrepiece of this 'hymn to Christ' is his death, to be more precise, his crucifixion—'death on a cross'. Paul is declaring that God the Son became a slave, but in his death he became a curse. In the one he descended to earth, in the other he descended to hell. Here, then, is the very heartbeat of God's mission in Jesus to his creatures living 'under the sun'—to bear away their guilt by absorbing into his pure and sinless body the divine wrath we deserve because of our impure and sinful acts. This is the divine rescue which plumbs the pitiful depths of divine condescension, as stripped naked, bruised and bleeding, his shame is displayed before the whole world to see—God's own Son nailed to a cross and left to die. It is supremely at the cross of Christ that we see the judgement anticipated by the Teacher, 'God will bring to judgement both the righteous and the wicked, for there will be a time for every activity, a time for every deed.' This was the time of God's greatest deed—to re-connect to himself those who have gone astray and who by themselves cannot discern any purpose under heaven.

Dorothy L. Sayers, in her own inimitable way, spells out what this means for our understanding of God and his relationship to us living in the world of Ecclesiastes:

For whatever reason God chose to make man as he is—limited and suffering and subject to sorrows and death—He had the honesty and the courage to take His own medicine. Whatever game He is playing with His creation, He has kept His own rules and played fair. He has Himself gone through the whole of human experience, from the trivial irritations of family life and lack of money to the worst horrors, pain, humiliation, defeat, despair and death. He was born in poverty and died in disgrace and felt it was all worthwhile.[141]

It *was* God they crucified instead of you and me.

What is more, he was also raised from the dead for you and me. The futility of life against the backcloth of the inevitability of death permeates the whole of Ecclesiastes and it lies just below the surface of what Paul says elsewhere concerning the coming of Christ to reverse the futility caused by death as Jesus died and rose for us:

> When the perishable has been clothed with immortality, [here Paul is looking to the future resurrection of those who have put their trust in Christ and his death and resurrection], then the saying that is written will come true: 'Where, O death, is your victory? Where, O death, is your sting?' The sting of death is sin, and the power of sin is the law. But thanks be to God! He gives us the victory through our Lord Jesus Christ. Therefore, my dear brothers, stand firm. Let nothing move you. Always give yourselves fully to the work of the Lord, because you know that your labour in the Lord is not in *vain* [the Greek word for *hebel*—vapour] (1 Corinthians 15:54–58).

Because death is not the end for believers, life takes on a

significance not envisaged by the Qoheleth, a significance which will culminate in an 'eternal weight of glory' (2 Corinthians 4:17).[142]

A time to dance

How does Jesus, the Teacher *par excellence*, the one 'greater than Solomon' turn mourning into dancing? Let the story of what happened to Bessie Ship show how.

Bessie Ship who was spending Christmas in an American prison as she was dying of AIDS. She went along to a Christmas service in the jail. Afterwards she said to the man leading the service that she wanted to know Jesus too. So there and then she gave her life to Christ in prayer. Going home as a fresh Christian was a new experience for her. She was immediately drawn into a church and nurtured in the faith as she went to a Bible study group. Just three weeks after she had been released she contracted pneumonia. In hospital a Christian minister visited her. Struggling, she whispered to him, 'These have been the happiest days of my life to know Jesus loves me, and that you do too.' Two days later she died. She went to meet the Saviour she had accepted on Christmas day in a cold prison cell.[143]

When the Son of God came to earth, he wasn't born in a warm palace, but a dirty backroom which doubled as a stable reeking of animal dung and urine. And by his Spirit he still comes to us, wherever we are, whoever we are. Not just to inhabit dark and cold buildings, but dark and lost souls.

Jesus came to turn mourning into dancing, tears into laughter. This world of vapour is passing away, but what Jesus, the Son of David, the Qoheleth, the Son of God is bringing into being will last for ever.

Questions for further thought and discussion

Think about the darkest and happiest times of your life. What were the range of emotions you experienced? Now think through Jesus' life and how he experienced those emotions too.

In what ways does knowing Jesus enable us to experience joy in our life 'under Heaven' while we still experience the sorrow of life 'under the sun'?

Think back over our journey with the Teacher and the realities of life we've explored. Are there parts of your life and experience in this world that you need to give over to Christ to forgive, transform and heal? Perhaps think about your emotional life, experience of death and suffering, work, pleasure and unanswered questions about the world.

Notes

1. Robert K. Johnston, *Useless Beauty. Ecclesiastes through the lens of Contemporary Film* (Grand Rapids, Michigan: Baker Academic Press, 2004), p. 20.

2. Cited by Michael Green, in *Critical Choices* (Leicester: IVP, 1995) p. 17.

3. Leo Tolstoy, *Confessions* (Penguin Books, 1987), p. 26.

4. Tom Wolfe, 'God's Lonely Man' in *The Hills Beyond* (New York: Plume/New American Library, 1982), pp. 146, 148. Interestingly enough, Tom Wolfe described Ecclesiastes as 'the greatest single piece of writing I have ever known.'

5. Robert K. Johnston, *Useless Beauty. Ecclesiastes through the lens of Contemporary Film* (Grand Rapids, Michigan: Baker Academic Press, 2004), p. 179.

6. 'Qoheleth's [*the writer of Ecclesiastes*] God may be detected not so much by sight as by scent and footprint, but he is unquestionably present nonetheless. Scholars have sometimes missed this important foundation for Ecclesiastes, believing the book to be secular in its orientation. But this is a mistake. It is true that Qoheleth uses the generic term for God, Elohim, rather than the more personal and distinctly Hebraic name, Yahweh. It is true that God is perceived as distant. But according to Qoheleth God makes everything (11:5)—the beautiful (3:11) and the

crooked (7:13), the good and the bad times (7:14), he gives humankind the days of their lives (5:18; 8:15), their spirit or breath (12:7), their work (5:19–20), their wealth (6:2) and their sustenance (2:24–26), he also gives burdens (1:13). God tests people (3:18) and will judge (11:9), taking no pleasure in fools (5:4) and calling the past into account (3:14). Though clearly present in all life, God is also incomprehensible to Qoheleth. God is heaven, and we are on earth (5:2). We cannot know what he has done (3:11).' Robert K. Johnston, *Useless Beauty*, p. 175.

7.   John H. Walton and Andrew E. Hill, Old Testament Today: A Journey from Original Meaning to Contemporary Significance (Grand Rapids: Zondervan, 2004), p. 312.

8.   Barry Webb, *Five Festal Garments: Christian Reflections on The Song of Songs, Ruth, Lamentations, Ecclesiastes and Esther* (Leicester: Apollos, 2000), p. 83.

9.   Peter Enns, 'Ecclesiastes according to the Gospel: Christian Thoughts on Qohelet's Theology', *Scripture and Interpretation*, 2:1 (2008): pp. 25–38 [25].

10.   Craig G. Bartholomew, 'The Theology of Ecclesiastes'; in *The Words of the Wise are like Goads: Engaging Qohelet in the 21st Century*, Edited by Mark J. Boda, Tremper Longman III and Cristian G. Rata (Winona Lake, Indiana: Eisenbrauns, 2013), p. 363.

11.   G. K. Chesterton, 'What's Wrong with the World?' in *G. K. Chesterton, The Apostle of Common Sense*, ed. Dale Ahlquist, (Ignatius Press, 2003), p. 43.

12.   'The verb 'to see' (*ra'ah*) is used 47 times in his short reflection. Readers are encouraged to see life honestly yet paradoxically—not only its bleakness and mystery but also as something worthy of enjoyment.'— Johnston, *Useless Beauty*, p. 174.

13.   The Hebrew root of *qohelet* is '*qahal*', the equivalent Greek word, is '*ecclesia*', hence the title of the book, 'Ecclesiastes', which comes from the Septuagint (The Greek translation of the Old Testament).

14.   Jonathan Sacks, *The Great Partnership: God, Science and the Search for Meaning*, (London: Hodder and Stoughton, 2011), p. 41.

15.   'Such texts as Job, Ecclesiastes, and the parables do not function primarily as raw material for Christian doctrine ... Their primary function is to invite or to provoke the reader to wrestle actively with issues, in ways that may involve adopting a series of comparative angles of vision.' Anthony Thiselton, *New Horizons in Hermeneutics: The Theory and Practice of Transforming Bible Reading* (Grand Rapids, MI: Zondervan, 1997) pp. 55–57.

16.   For example: W. C. Kaiser, Jr., *Ecclesiastes: Total Life* in Everyman's Bible Commentary; (Chicago: Moody Press, 1979).

17.   Tremper Longman III argues that Qoheleth adopts the persona of Solomon (Ecclesiastes 1:12–6:9) so as to explore avenues of meaning in the world. King Solomon might be considered to have been in the best position to evaluate life. He had it all: money, girls, wisdom and a kingdom—maybe, Qoheleth thinks, Solomon might shed some light on life. So Qoheleth is not Solomon, he is simply using him as a fictive teaching device to explore certain avenues about life under the sun. Tremper Longman III, *The Book of Ecclesiastes* in New International Commentary on the Old Testament (Grand Rapids: Eerdmans, 1998), pp. 6–8; 15–20.

18.   Iain Provan, *Ecclesiastes, Song of Songs* (The NIV Application Commentary; Grand Rapids: Zondervan, 2001), p51. Peter J. Leithart writes, 'When the word is used metaphorically, it emphasises the ephemerality and elusiveness of human existence. Human life is *hebel* (Psalm 39:4–11; Job 7:16) because it is impermanent, because we change and ultimately die. Words (Job 21:34) and beauty (Proverbs 31:30) are "mere breath" for the same reason. When Solomon describes everything as vapour, he's not saying that everything is meaningless and pointless. He's highlighting the elusiveness of the world, which slips though our fingers and escapes all our efforts to manage it.' Peter J. Leithart, *Solomon*

among the Postmoderns (Grand Rapids, Michigan: Brazos Press, 2008), p. 67.

19. 'What Qohelet means in the opening chapters of the book is that seeking refuge in wealth and possessions, or even in books and wisdom, is futile since life is no more than a fleeting breath. Ecclesiastes is a sustained meditation on the vulnerability of life. Hevel, a shallow breath, is all that separates the living from the dead. We live, we die, and it is as if we have never been. We build, and others occupy. We accumulate possessions, but others enjoy them. The good we do is soon forgotten. The wisdom we acquire is useless, for it merely brings us back to the recognition of our own mortality. To seek happiness in objects that endure is a kind of self-deception: they last, we do not.' Sacks, *The Great Partnership*, p. 189.

20. Enns, 'Ecclesiastes According to the Gospel', p. 28.

21. Ibid. p. 27.

22. Henry David Thoreau, *Walden* (Oxford World Classics, 2008), ch.1.

23. Francis Schaeffer and Koop C. Everett, *Whatever Happened to the Human Race?* (London: Marshall, Morgan and Scott, 1980), pp. 97–98.

24. Stig Björkman, *Woody Allen on Woody Allen* (New York: Grove Press, 1993).

25. Walton and Hill, *Old Testament Today*, p. 312.

26. 'A particular challenge for interpreters is the fact that Qohelet clings tenaciously to both claims: all life is *hebel*, and yet joy is both possible and good. It is important not to make one of these claims the only message of the book and dismiss the other either as a distraction or a grudging qualification. Qohelet insists on both, and often in the same passage. Thus any interpretation that attempts to separate them or exclude one is a distortion.' 'Ecclesiastes' in Roland E. Murphy and Elizabeth Huwiler, *Proverbs, Ecclesiastes, Song of Songs*, New International Bible Commentary, Old Testament, vol. 12 (Peabody, Massachusetts: Hendrickson, 1999), p165. While this challenge is proper, one cannot

avoid the clear 'in your face' repetition of the term *hebel*, which does seem to be the guiding principle throughout the book and a check on whatever good we enjoy. The corrective is necessary that while we live in this world which is littered with so many 'goods' coming from the gracious hand of a generous God, we are not to get too attached to it, for 1. It won't last and 2. It can lead us into idolatry and away from our Maker.

27. Johnston, *Useless Beauty,* pp. 28–29

28. 'Verses 5–7 are an extended illustration where the narrator appeals to creation in support of his summary. Unlike the Psalter, which praises God for his creation, Qohelet sees creation as confirming the futility of existence. The sun rises and sets, every day the same thing (v. 5). The image drawn here is of the sun rising, setting, and then "panting" to get back in place in order to do it all again the next day. But what is in it for the sun? What profit does the sun have? Its existence is absurd, just like ours. It is as if Qohelet is saying, "You don't believe all of life is absurd? Just look out the window." The same goes for the wind (v. 6). From north to south, round and round it goes on its rounds, a never-ending cycle. Then, in v. 7, we see how the rivers flow into the ocean, but for all their hard work, the oceans are never full: there is no profit.' Enns, 'Ecclesiastes According to the Gospel', p. 29.

29. Leithart, *Solomon among the Postmoderns*, pp. 127–8.

30. Enns, 'Ecclesiastes According to the Gospel', p. 30.

31. 'The scientific quest found fertile soil *only* when faith in a personal, rational Creator had truly permeated a whole culture, beginning with the centuries of the High Middle Ages. It was that faith which provided, in sufficient measure, confidence in the rationality of the universe, trust in progress, and an appreciation of the qualitative method, all indispensable ingredients of the scientific quest.' Stanley L. Jaki, *Science and Creation* (Lanham: University Press of America, 1990).

32. Cited by Os Guinness, *Long Journey Home: A Guide to Your Search for the Meaning of Life* (Colorado Springs: Waterbrook Press, 2001), p. 28.

33.   This perspective prevents us from identifying the position of the Teacher with that of atheistic philosophers like Russell. Commenting on this important distinction, Graeme Goldsworthy writes, 'Qohelet's cry of utter meaninglessness is not of the same order. To begin with, he is convinced of the reality of God and of meaning which is known to God. That there is a personal, creator God makes it possible for us mortals to grasp life as his gift, and that alone gives reality meaning.' Graeme Goldsworthy, *Gospel and Wisdom: Israel's Wisdom Literature in the Christian Life* (Carlisle: Paternoster Press, 1995), p. 108.

34.   Walton and Hill, *Old Testament Today*, p. 313.

35.   Ravi Zacharias, *Can Man Live without God?* (Nashville: Thomas Nelson, 1994), p. 58.

36.   Harry Blamires, *Where Do We Stand? An Examination of the Christian's Position in the Modern World.* (London: SPCK, 1980), p. 50.

37.   Ibid. p. 53

38.   Ibid. p. 54.

39.   Ibid. p. 58.

40.   Ibid. p. 59.

41.   Jonathan Sacks, *The Great Partnership: God, Science and the Search for Meaning* (London: Hodder and Stoughton, 2011), p. 200.

42.   Os Guinness, *Fit Bodies Fat Minds: Why Evangelicals Don't Think and What to Do About It* (Hodder and Stoughton, 1995), pp. 89–94.

43.   Peter J. Leithart, *Solomon among the Postmoderns* (Grand Rapids, Michigan: Brazos Press, 2008), p. 127.

44.   Pete Lowman, *A Long Way East of Eden: Could God Explain the Mess We're In?* (Carlisle: Paternoster, 2002), p. 22.

45.   Tim Keller, *The Freedom of Self-forgetfulness: The Pathway to True Christian Joy* (Chorley: 10publishing, 2012), p. 22.

46.   Kenne Fant, *Alfred Nobel: A Biography* (New York: Arcade Publishing, 1991) p. 1.

47.   Sacks, The Great Partnership, p. 203.

48. Sacks, The Great Partnership, p. 204.

49. Os Guinness, *The Long Journey Home* (Colorado Springs: Waterbrook Press, 2001), p. 50.

50. Cited by David F. Wells, *Above All Earthly Powers,*(IVP, 2005), p. 179.

51. Os Guinness, *The Long Journey Home* (Colorado: Waterbrook Press, 2001), p. 29.

52. Graham Lord, *Niv: The Authorised Biography of David Niven* (Orion, 2003).

53. A. R. Eckardt, 'The Recantation of the Covenant' in A. H. Rosenfeld and I. Greenberg, Eds, *Confronting the Holocaust: The Impact of Elie Wiesel* (Bloomington: Indiana University Press), p. 163.

54. Aldous Huxley, *Ends and Means* (London: Chatto & Windus, 1946), p. 273.

55. Leszek Kołakowski, *Religion* (London, Fontana, 1982) p. 215.

56. Peter Berger, *A Rumour of Angels: Modern Society and the Rediscovery of the Supernatural* (New York: Anchor Books, 1969).

57. Robert K. Johnston, *Useless Beauty. Ecclesiastes through the lens of Contemporary Film* (Grand Rapids, Michigan: Baker Academic Press, 2004), p. 176.

58. Os Guinness, *Long Journey Home* (Colorado Springs: Waterbrook Press, 2001), p. 27.

59. Os Guinness, *Unspeakable—Facing Up to Evil in an Age of Genocide and Terror* (Harper Collins, 2005), p.217.

60. Ludwig Wittgenstein, *Tractatus logico-philosophicus,* (London, 1922), 6:41.

61. Jonathan Sacks, *The Great Partnership: God, Science and the Search for Meaning* (Hodder and Stoughton, 2011) p. 29.

62. David Myers, *The American Paradox: Spiritual Hunger in an Age of Plenty* (Yale University Press, 2001).

63. Greg Easterbrook, *The Progress Paradox: How Life Gets Better While People Feel Worse* (Random House, 2003).

64. Mike Starkey, *Born to Shop* (Monarch, 1989), p. 83.

65. Jonathan Sacks, *The Great Partnership: God, Science and the Search for Meaning* (London: Hodder and Stoughton, 2011), p. 279.

66. Ibid. p. 191.

67. John H. Walton and Andrew E. Hill, *Old Testament Today: A Journey from Original Meaning to Contemporary Significance* (Grand Rapids: Zondervan, 2004), p. 330.

68. Os Guinness, 'The Word in the Age of the Image—A Challenge to Evangelicals' in *The Anglican Evangelical Crisis,* Ed. Melvin Tinker (Fearn: Christian Focus Publications, 1995), p. 168.

69. Os Guinness, *Prophetic Timeliness—A Challenge to the Idol of Relevance* (Baker Books, 2003), pp. 110–111.

70. Charles Colson, *Against the Night* (Servant Publications, 1999), pp. 116.

71. Jonathan Aitken, *Charles W. Colson: A Life Redeemed* (London: Continuum, 2005).

72. Ibid. p. 117.

73. I owe this summary to Peter Lewis of Cornerstone Church, Nottingham.

74. Jonathan Sacks, *The Great Partnership: God, Science and the Search for Meaning* (London: Hodder and Stoughton, 2011), p.135.

75. See Melvin Tinker, *Road to Reality: Finding Meaning in a Meaningless World* (Christian Focus, 2004), p. 57.

76. Dale Ralph Davis, *2 Kings; The Power and Fury* (Fearn: Christian Focus, 2009), p. 22.

77. For a thorough treatment of this subject see Melvin Tinker, *Intended for Good: The Providence of God* (Inter Varsity Press, 2012).

78. The term translated 'Kingdom of God', *Basileia tou theou*—can be translated the 'Government of God' or the 'Reign of God', but in the New

Testament it signifies more than 'God reigns', it is that sphere of God's rule in which there is eternal life. Jesus is the King of God's kingdom. See David Seccombe's excellent treatment—*The King of God's Kingdom: A Solution to the Puzzle of Jesus* (Authentic Media, 2002).

79. Cited by Charles Colson, *Against the Night* (Servant Publications, 1999), p. 120.

80. Russell Kirk, 'The Wise Men Know What Wicked things Are Written in the Sky,' *Modern Age* (Spring 1985), p. 113.

81. D. M. Lloyd-Jones, 'The Christian and The State in Revolutionary Times', *The Puritans: Their Origins and Their Successors* (Banner of Truth Trust, 1987), pp. 342–343.

82. Ibid. p. 341.

83. On John Wesley's understanding of the relations between the need for conversion and social transformation, J. Bready writes: 'As a prophet of God and an ordained ambassador of Christ, he did not conceive it his task to formulate economic, political and social theories; nor did he judge himself competent so to do. His "calling" he believed was far more sacred, and more thoroughgoing: it was to lead men into contact with spiritual reality, to enable them to possess their souls and enter the realms of abundant life. For if once men, in sufficient numbers, were endowed with an illumined conscience and spiritual insight they, collectively as well as individually, would become possessors of the "wisdom that passeth knowledge"; and in that wisdom social problems gradually would be solved.' J. Wesley Bready, *England Before and After Wesley* (Hodder and Stoughton, 1939), p. 257.

84. Élie Halévy, *The Triumph of Reform 1830–1841—a History of the English People in the Nineteenth Century Vol 3* (Penguin, 1931), p. 85.

85. Jack Lawson, *A Man's Life* (Hodder and Stoughton, 1932), p. 66.

86. For a more extended treatment of the relationship between the Gospel and Christian Social Involvement see, Melvin Tinker, 'Reversal or Betrayal? Evangelicals and Socio-Political Involvement in the

Twentieth Century', in *Evangelical Concerns* (Mentor: Christian Focus Publications, 2001), pp. 139–166; 'The Servant Solution: The co-ordination of evangelism and social action. The John Wenham lecture 2006'— *Themelios, Vol 32, Issue 2, 2007* and 'Ministries of Mercy, Moral Distance and the Parable of the Good Samaritan—the Challenge to Evangelical Social Action'—*Churchman, 123/1,2009.*

87.   D. A. Carson, *How Long O Lord? Reflections on Suffering and Evil* (Inter Varsity Press, 1990), p. 15.

88.   Elie Wiesel, *Night* (Penguin 1981).

89.   Gordon Reece, 'Ethics and the End of Life', in *The Ethics of Life and Death* Ed. Barry Webb (Explorations 4, Lancer, 1990), p. 108.

90.   Os Guinness, *Unspeakable—Facing up to Evil in an Age of Genocide* (Harper/Collins, 2005), p. 53.

91.   Ibid. p. 54.

92.   His approach to the tragedy and the seemingly meaninglessness of it all is reminiscent of the Qoheleth, 'Since I knew that darkness was inevitable and unavoidable, I decided from that point on to walk into the darkness rather than try and outrun it, to let my experience of loss take me on a journey wherever it would lead, and to allow myself to be transformed by my suffering rather than think I could somehow avoid it.' Jerry Sittser, *A Grace Disguised: How the Soul Grows through Loss* (Grand Rapids, MI: Zondervan, 2004), p. 42.

93.   Os Guinness, *Unspeakable—Facing up to Evil in an Age of Genocide* (Harper/ Collins, 2005) pp. 56–57.

94.   For a full treatment of this subject see, Melvin Tinker, *Why Bad things Happen to Good People?* (Christian Focus, 2009).

95.   John Hick, 'An Irenaean Theodicy' *Encountering Evil*, S. T. Davies Ed. (T. and T. Clark 1981) pp. 38–52.

96.   C. S. Lewis, *A Grief Observed*, (Fount 1962).

97.   Harold S. Kushner, *When Bad Things Happen to Good People* (Anchor; Reprint edition, 2004).

98. Philip Yancey, *Where is God when it Hurts?* (Zondervan, 1977).

99. 'The early chapters of Genesis represent the single most important influence on the ideas of Ecclesiastes regarding the nature and destiny of man, the character of human existence, and the fact of God.' C. C. Foreman, 'Koheleth's Use of Genesis'. *Journal of Semitic Studies 5* (1956), p. 263.

100. For a developed treatment of God's Providence see Melvin Tinker, *Intended for Good: The Providence of God* (Inter Varsity Press, 2012).

101. Michael A. Eaton, *Ecclesiastes: An Introduction and Commentary* (Inter Varsity Press, 1983), p. 70.

102. Guinness, *Unspeakable*, p. 66.

103. Os Guinness, *Doubt: Faith in Two Minds* (Inter Varsity Press, 1976), p. 209.

104. Nick Spencer, *Darwin and God*, (SPCK, 2009).

105. I owe this illustration to Peter Lewis of Cornerstone Church, Nottingham.

106. J. R. R. Tolkien, *The Hobbit or There and Back Again,* (Harper Collins, 2012).

107. Professor Paul Helm argues that the place of wisdom in bringing about knowledge of God and ourselves to enable us to get through life was the 'Big idea' of the 16th-century John Calvin. In the opening section of his *Institutes*, Calvin writes: 'Nearly all the wisdom we possess, that is to say, true and sound wisdom, consists in two parts; the knowledge of God and of ourselves. But, while joined by many bonds, which one precedes and brings forth the other is not easy to discern'. Helm remarks: 'The Christian religion offers a method of possessing true and sound wisdom. Here Calvin taps into one medieval emphasis, that the Christian religion has to do with the imparting of wisdom, *sapientia*, and he implicitly rejects another medieval emphasis, that theology has to do with theoretical understanding and certainty, *scientia* … Theology does not provide us with more knowledge in the form of more explanations,

as nuclear physics and astronomy and criminal detection do, but with wisdom. It has to do with the knowledge of God, certainly, but with that sort of knowledge that enables us to enjoy the favour and presence of God, and to bring us to our everlasting home.' *The John Murray Lecture* delivered at the Highland Theological College, Dingwall, Scotland, on March 6th 2008, cited in 'Helm's Deep' April 1st 2008 http://paulhelmsdeep.blogspot.co.uk/2008/04/john-calvin-whats-big-idea.html

108. See Melvin Tinker, *Intended for Good—The Providence of God* (IVP, 2012), Chapter 8.

109. Robert K. Johnston, *Useless Beauty. Ecclesiastes through the lens of Contemporary Film* (Grand Rapids, Michigan: Baker Academic Press, 2004), p. 165.

110. See for example the conclusion Ecclesiastes 12:12, 'Be warned my *son,* of anything in addition to them.'

111. Iain Provan, *Ecclesiastes and the Song of Songs, The New Application Commentary* (Zondervan, 2001), p. 194. Alternatively: 'Dead flies could also means "poisonous flies," which opens the possibility that the fermented perfume may even become toxic.', Craig Bartholomew, *Ecclesiastes,* (Baker, Grand Rapids, Michigan, 2009), pp. 320–321. In both cases the application is the same; despite the perfume, what lies underneath is unhealthy.

112. James H. Jones, *Kinsey: A life* (W. W. Norton & Company, 2004).

113. I owe this helpful illustration to John Piper—Sex and the Supremacy of Christ—Desiring God Ministries.

114. William J. Donnelly, *The Confetti Generation: How the New Communications Technology Is Fragmenting America* (Henry Holt & Co, 1986)

115. T. S. Eliot, *Choruses from the Rock*, 1934.

116. Charles Colson, *Against the Night: Living in the New Dark Ages,* (Vine Books, 1991), p. 108.

117. Rodney Stark, *The Rise of Christianity. A sociologist reconsiders history* (Princeton University Press, 1996), p. 161.

118. Jonathan Aitken, *Nixon—A Life* (Regnery Publishers, 1993).

119. Releasing bread upon the water is 'a figure taken from the corn trade of a seaport ... an illustration of the thought: seek thy support in the way of bold, confident adventure.' F. Delitzsch, *Proverbs, Ecclesiastes, Song of Solomon*. Translated by M. G. Easton. (Grand Rapids: Eerdmans, 1975).

120. 'The process by which sectors of society and culture are removed from the domination of religious institutions and symbols.' Peter L. Berger, *The Sacred Canopy: Elements of a Sociological Theory of Religion* (Garden City: Doubleday, 1967), p. 107. Similarly Bryan Wilson defines secularisation as 'the process whereby religious thinking, practice and institutions lose their social significance', quoted *in Bryan Wilson, Religion in Secular Society: A Sociological Comment* (London: Watts, 1966), p. 14.

121. Cited in Os Guinness, *Dining with the Devil: The Mega-Church Movement Flirts with Modernity* (Grand Rapids: Baker, 1993), p. 49.

122. J. William Jones, *Christ in the Camp* (Harrisonburg, Virginia: Sprinkle Publications, 1986), p. 90.

123. Jerry Bridges, *Respectable Sins*, (NavPress, 2007), p. 66.

124. Jennifer Worth, *In the Midst of Life* (Phoenix, 2012), p. 45.

125. This is the fair conclusion the narrator draws from what the Qoheleth has been arguing, 'Qoheleth demonstrates the futility of trying to find meaning in a fallen world apart from remembering one's Creator and beginning with the fear of the Lord, but he also affirms life, and he resolves the tension at the conclusion of his journey precisely through his exhortation to remember one's Creator. Thus, the futility that Ecclesiastes exposes is the attempt to find meaning while embracing human autonomy in a world that depends at every point on its Creator', Craig G. Bartholomew, 'The Theology of Ecclesiastes', in *The Words of the Wise are like Goads: Engaging Qohelet in the 21st Century*, Edited by

Mark J. Boda, Tremper Longman III and Cristian G. Rata (Winona Lake, Indiana: Eisenbrauns, 2013), pp. 380–381.

126. Lewis Smedes, *How can it be all right when everything is all wrong?* (San Francisco: Harper and Row, 1982).

127. Dorothy L. Sayers, 'The Dogma is the Drama' in *Creed or Chaos?* (New York: Harcourt, Brace and Co, 1949), pp. 20–24.

128. Athanasius, *On the Incarnation* (Crestwood New York: St Vladimir's Seminary Press, 1996) p. 45.

129. Augustine, Sermon 187 1.1

130. This is referred to as the *'extra-Calvinisticus' Institutes of John Calvin, 2:13:4,* Ed. John Thomas McNeill (Westminster/John Knox, USA 2001).

131. Richard Bauckham, *Jesus and the Eyewitnesses: the Gospels as eyewitness testimony* (Grand Rapids, Michigan: William B. Eerdmans, 2006).

132. 'Those calling upon Jesus and his friends to fast are moving in the wrong direction, for, in fact, the coming of Jesus is more like a funeral that is turned into a wedding banquet … Isaiah looked forward to a great time of feasting at the end of the ages, when God would do away with death and mourning and tears and spread out a banquet for his people (Isaiah 25:6–8). This is a picture of future resurrection life (cf. 26:19), for God promised that on this day he would remove the shroud of death that covers the nations and swallow up death forever. Mourning will be abolished, for resurrection life will have come!' Peter Bolt, *The Cross from a Distance. Atonement in Mark's Gospel* (Illinois: Apollos, IVP, 2004), p. 23.

133. N. Wolterstorff, *Until Justice and Peace Embrace*: The Kuyper Lectures for 1981 Delivered at the Free University of Amsterdam (Grand Rapids: Eerdmans, 193) p. 69.

134. 'Ecclesiastes' happiness—another key word of the book, as it is of the Hebrew Bible generally—is *simchah*, which means, "joy, celebration,

exuberance" ... Ecclesiastes' vision of the good life is simply happier than that of the Greeks of the third pre-Christian century, and this too has something to do with the basic attitude of trust.' and 'Happiness in the Bible is not something we find in self-gratification. Hence the significance of the word *simchah*. I translated it earlier as "joy", but really it has no precise translation into English, since all our emotion words refer to states of mind we can experience alone. *Simchah* is something we cannot experience alone. *Simchah* is joy shared.' Jonathan Sacks, *The Great Partnership: God, Science and the Search for Meaning* (London: Hodder and Stoughton, 2011), p. 191 and p. 204.

135. Anderson and Foley remind us 'how much of his ministry is remembered through the food and dining metaphors that provide the vernacular for narrating the Jesus event. His food was the will of the one he called father, and this divine will, in turn, became the enduring banquet for any who dared to follow him. Jesus' ministry, his evangelising, his legacy were so intimately linked to the ritual metaphors of dining and food that, in his fascinating book *Six Thousand Years of Bread* (1944), H. E. Jacob could entitle his chapter on Jesus as "Jesus Christ: The Bread of God" ... And as remembered over and over again in the Gospels, they killed him because of the way he ate; that is, because he ate and drank with sinners.' H. Anderson and E. Foley, *Mighty Stories, Dangerous Rituals: Weaving Together the Human and Divine* (San Francisco: Jossey-Bass, 1988) p. 155. We might also add that it is significant that one of the things Jesus commanded his followers to do was to have a regular meal in remembrance of him—the Lord's Supper.

136. John 10:35

137. So argues Craig Bartholomew, *Ecclesiastes* (Baker, Grand Rapids, Michigan, 2009), p. 382.

138. The writer Karl Barth notes how enjoying life is a common theme in the Bible and especially more so in the light of the coming of Jesus, 'it is now genuine, earthly, human joy; the joy of the harvest, wedding, festival

and victory; the joy not only of the inner but also the outer man; the joy in which one may and must drink wine as well as eat bread, sing and play as well as speak, dance as well as pray ... We must also remember that the man who hears and takes to heart the Biblical message is not only permitted but plainly forbidden to be anything but merry and cheerful.' Karl Barth, *Church Dogmatics* 3:4; 374–84 (Edited by G. W. Bromiley and T. F. Torrance, T&T Clark, 2004).

139. C. S. Lewis, *Surprised by Joy* (Harcourt, Brace, Jovanovich; 15th Edition 1966), pp. 222–223.

140. At the baptism of Jesus we are presented with a similar picture of the Trinity (Matthew 3:16–17) as joy. Commenting on this, Michael Reeves writes: 'For in making the loving Father of lights known, the Spirit is the bringer not only of love but of joy and is regularly associated with joy next to which the merriness of wine is no substitute (Ephesians 5:18; see also Galatians 5:22; Romans 14:17) in *Delighting in the Trinity: An Introduction to the Christian Faith* (Illinois: VP Academic Downer Grove, 2012), p. 30.

141. Dorothy L. Sayers, 'The Dogma is the Drama' in *Creed or Chaos?* (New York: Harcourt, Brace and Co, 1949), pp. 20–24.

142. 'For Christians, the ultimate context for Ecclesiastes is the entire Christian Bible, both the Old and New Testaments. Thus the complete canon witnesses to Jesus Christ as God's final saving word ... some of the aspects of this book [Ecclesiastes], which point to the disordered, chaotic, fallen aspects of existence, serve as an Old Testament dramatic foil to the really "new thing" that has happened in Jesus Christ. Whereas in Ecclesiastes there is the forceful reminder that there is nothing new under the sun, in the completed Christian canon there can now be heard the message of the One who will make all things new (Revelation 21:5). Whereas the spectre of death and disorder and curse haunts the book of Ecclesiastes from beginning to end, the Christian now hears the words of a greater than Solomon who enters the disorientation, tastes death for every person, and leaves the tomb empty, his final sign for an old history:

death is being swallowed up by resurrection life (John 11:25). Whereas "vanity" had cast its shadow over everything, the resurrection of Christ assures the believer that nothing done in the Lord will ever be in vain (1 Corinthians 15:58). Whereas judgement looms ominously after death for Ecclesiastes, the dreaded judgement has fallen upon Christ, and there is now the unbelievably good news of the cross, because Christ took upon himself all the labour of a cursed world (Romans 1:20; 2 Corinthians 5:21, Hebrews 10:19). The motto at the end of the book about fearing God (which is the essence of humanity) now appears as the ultimate object of this fear: Christ, the Wisdom of God.' Stephen G. Dempster, 'Ecclesiastes and the Canon' in *The Words of the Wise are like Goads: Engaging Qohelet in the 21st Century*, Edited by Mark J. Boda, Tremper Longman III and Cristian G. Rata (Winona Lake, Indiana: Eisenbrauns, 2013), p. 399. Similarly, Peter J. Leithart writes, 'the Christian faith is that the Word who is the beginning and the end, the Word who became flesh, has already swallowed up death in life by his own resurrection from the dead. Christian faith is the faith of the eternal Word, the Word that is the first and the last word, the alpha word that spoke the creation into being and the omega word that pronounces all very good, this eternal Word who is with God and who is God, has taken flesh and dwelt amongst us. After the shards and fragments of revelation through the prophets, God has spoken to us in his Son: he has spoken the Word that is his Son, his final word (Hebrews 1:1–2), into the world. Within this world under the sun, there is a Word from the world beyond the world under the sun, and that Word stands forever.' in *Solomon among the Postmoderns* (Brazos Press, Grand Rapids, Michigan, 2008) pp. 101–102.

143. Charles Colson, *A Dangerous Grace* (Nelson Word Ltd, 1994), p. 478.